The
A Happy Pet

Creating A Loving Bond

Kelly O'Tillery

© 2019 ETC Publishing

All rights reserved. No part of this book may be reproduced or transmitted in any form or by any means, electronic or mechanical including photocopying or recording, or by any information storage and retrieval system without written permission from the author and publisher, except in the case of brief quotations embodied in critical reviews and articles.

Published by ETC Publishing
Carlsbad, California
WWW.ETCPUBLISHING.COM

First Edition, First Publication 2019

ISBN: 978-1-944622-27-5

Cover design by Gary Dunham and Kelly O'Tillery

Although every precaution has been taken in the preparation of this book, the publisher and author assume no responsibility for errors or omissions. Neither is any liability assumed for damages resulting from the use of the information contained herin.

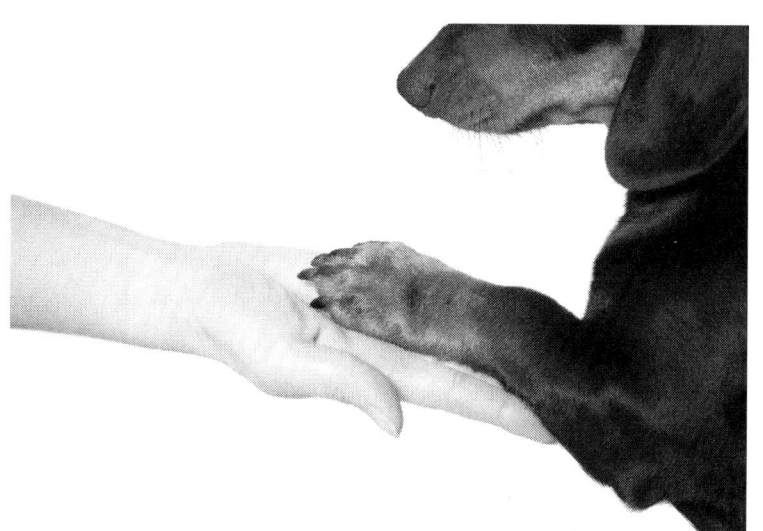

Contents

Introduction 7
Things to Consider Before You Adopt a Pet 11
Popular Pets 16
Communication Between You and Your Pet 19
Illness 21
Miscommunication Between You and Your Pet 25
An Agreement Between You and Your Pet 27
Emergency or Natural Disaster 35
Legal Documents Involving Your Pet 37
Living Agreements 38
A Dog for Companionship 42
A Cat for Companionship 47
A Bird for Companionship 51
A Pet Snake 55
A Dog for the Family 59
A Cat for the Family 64
A Rabbit for the Family 68
Guinea Pigs for the Family 72
A Guard Dog for Personal Protection 76
A Dog for Show and Breeding 80
Service Dogs 85
A Guide Dog 88
More Information about Pets in this Book 92
Questions and Answers 98
A Staycation for Your Pet 104
About Kelly O'Tillery 109

Introduction

In my life I've been blessed to be able to welcome a number of people and pets into my heart. Each relationship has enriched my life on many levels and in different ways. I've always been curious about the relationships we create in certain aspects of our lives. Most of our relationships are built on an agreement between two or more of us, each bringing our special gifts, expectations, and experiences into the connection we will share with each other.

It seems each of these relationships and connections last when we are on the same page. Our agreement changes when those involved are no longer willing or able to continue in a way that satisfies each of our—in most cases—unspoken or evolving needs. Change happens regularly, and we mostly are aware we need to be flexible. If we want to maintain our relationships, we learn to shift, flow, and continue in them.

However, sometimes an agreement between us has subtle rules and expectations. These non-verbal agreements may be understood differently by the parties involved. This can lead to misunderstandings, struggles or unmet expectations.

For this reason, we may make a more official agreement—either by discussing and agreeing to the changed circumstances, or we draw up an agreement we both can commit to. I'd be surprised if you don't have at least a dozen such written and confirmed commitments/agreements (and even more based on a mutual understanding.)

When need or love is part of an agreement, we verbally communicate our hopes and wishes—perhaps more, we expect to outline and agree on some important parameters as we go along. Then we can formalize our agreement with a ceremony or a document which helps us remember our commitment to each other. In this instance our agreement is a gift and a treasure to us both, clearly defining and outlining the expectations and hopes each of us has. It's also a foundation for building a future, a way for each party to know they are protected by their mutual interest in one another's well-being.

In writing this book, I am bringing together the concept of an actual *"Agreement"* between ourselves and the pets we bring into our lives. I believe we give ourselves a gift by defining and outlining our own expectation of our pets as we commit to providing for their physical, mental, and emotional needs.

I will borrow the words of Saint Francis of Assisi who declared the animals who are a part of our world to be… "our brothers and sisters" in spirit. (Saint Francis of Assisi was born in 1182 and lived until 1226. His Feast Day is October 4th.)

Statue of Saint Francis outside the church in Puerto Villamil, Ecuador, in the Galapagos Islands January14,2015
ID 55621299 © Jesse Kraft/Dreamstime.com

I'll share one of my favorite stories about Saint Francis, one of the first people to show us how to relate with the creatures who share our space here on Earth. He believed that the world was created good and beautiful by God; he preached to man and beast the universal ability and duty of men to protect and enjoy nature as both the stewards of God's creation and as creatures ourselves.

One legend about this Saint tells about a city, Gubbio, where Francis lived for a time as a young priest in the Catholic Church. A ferocious wolf was terrifying the villagers… "devouring men as well as animals." Francis had compassion for the people of the town, so he went up into the hills to find the wolf.

The companions from the village who accompanied him on the search became fearful and fled back to town, but Francis continued searching until he found the wolf. When he did find it, he made the sign of the cross and commanded the wolf to come to him and cause him no harm.

The legend continues, saying that miraculously the wolf closed his jaws and lay down at the feet of St. Francis. "Brother Wolf, you do much harm to these parts," Francis explained. "All these people accuse you and curse you... But Brother Wolf, I would like to make peace between you and the people."

Then it is said that Francis walked with the wolf into the town. Surrounded by the shocked and startled people there, he made a pact between them and the wolf. Because the wolf had "caused harm out of hunger," the townspeople were to feed the wolf regularly.

In return, the wolf would no longer prey upon them or their flocks. Francis even made a pact on behalf of the town dogs: they would not bother the wolf again either. Then finally, to show the people they would no longer be harmed, Francis blessed the wolf.

Friar Francis was canonized Saint Francis by Pope Gregory IX in 1226 in Assisi, Italy, and on November 29, 1979 Pope John Paul II declared St. Francis the *Patron Saint of Ecology*. Around the world, churches are dedicated to Saint Francis of Assisi and to the spirit of his ministry. We often see statues and paintings of him surrounded by birds and smaller animals, some resting on his outstretched hands. Many of the legends and stories about him say he had a great love for animals and the environment.

It has become customary for Catholic and Anglican churches to hold ceremonies blessing animals on his feast day, October 4th. He is honored by the Church of England, the Anglican Church of Canada, The Episcopal Church USA, the Old Catholic Churches and the Evangelical Lutheran Church in America as well as many other churches and religious communities.

Saint Francis holds a place in my heart, and I have a statue of him by my hearth in the room where I did most of the writing for this book. I have shared the concepts I have written about in this book with friends and clients over the years, and now I hope you will find this little book helpful on a practical level, and as a useful tool or guide to enhance the relationship between you and the pets who are part of your life. I'd love to hear from you about your experiences.

Kelly O'Tillery

Things to Consider Before You Adopt a Pet

People adopt a pet or take in a stray animal with the best intentions, but good intentions must be balanced with the practical reality of caring for a pet. Throughout this book you'll find information encouraging you to think about many aspects of sharing your life with a pet.

People adopt a pet for a variety of reasons: companionship, for the family or a child, assistance with a physical disability or illness, emotional support, protection, for breeding or showing, etc. It's a good idea to ask yourself, "What is my motivation for adopting a pet?" Clarity regarding your desire for a pet will assist you in choosing the right pet, as well as improve the likelihood you and your pet will have a happy and mutually fulfilling relationship.

What are the expectations you have for a pet? Do you expect your pet to spend quiet time with you when you're relaxing after a long day at work? Maybe you want your pet to be your companion when you exercise: walking, running, hiking or other outdoor activities. Maybe you are homebound due to an illness or handicap, and you want a pet to help ease feelings of loneliness and isolation. Perhaps your children have been asking for a pet.

Some pets require a lot of supplies and/or equipment to create the environment or habitat they need to support their life. Before you bring a pet into your home, it's important to know what the pet will need right away and to be aware of what your pet will need long term. Consider whether the home you'll share will accommodate your pet's needs. Sadly, many pets are returned or taken to shelters because their owner cannot afford the cost of caring for the pet. Before you adopt or buy a pet, or take a stray animal home, consider all costs involved: adoption or purchase fee, food, accessories, healthcare, habitat, etc.

Lifestyle is also an important consideration. Do you live in a house with a big yard, or do you live in a small apartment or condo with no yard? Are your neighbors close enough to hear a dog barking or a noisy bird? Are there many pets in your neighborhood? Would you feel comfortable walking a dog in your neighborhood? Are you willing to adjust your schedule, routine, daily habits, and possibly social activities to create a happy and healthy relationship with your pet?

Think about your work schedule. Do you work full-time or part-time? How many hours a day are you away from home? Would your pet be home alone for many hours while you're at work? This is certainly a concern for very young animals, dogs, and some cats who may experience separation anxiety if left home alone.

At the end of your workday will you have time and energy to devote to your pet? This is a very important point to consider, as some animals and breeds require more attention, play, walks, mental stimulation, and exercise than others. Think about how much interaction you and/or your family members will have with a pet.

Will you be the primary guardian and caregiver for the pet? Do you have a partner or family members who will help with feeding, care, grooming, and exercise? Have you consulted with family members about adopting a pet? Do you have a baby, small children, or are you planning to become pregnant?

Do you know if any family members have allergies to animals, specifically to the type of pet you would like to adopt? If you or any family members have asthma, allergies or other health conditions, take the time to consult with a physician before adopting a pet.

It's vital you learn all you can about what the animal you plan to adopt needs—physical, mental, emotional, environmental—*before* you bring it home. If you're adopting a pet from a shelter or rescue organization find out what is known about the animal's history. How old is the animal? What is the adult size if the animal is young? Are they aware of any current health problems?

If you're adopting a dog, does it respond to basic commands like sit, stay, down, come, leave it? Has the dog been trained to walk on-leash? How does he or she respond to other animals—is it aggressive toward cats or frightened of other dogs? How does it respond to children? This is important information even if you don't have children.

Returning a pet to a shelter, breeder, pet store or previous owner is difficult for everyone, especially the animal. If you have questions, take time to check with your local Humane Society for information about a variety of pets before you choose one to take home with you.

Answers to the above questions will help you determine if an animal has been socialized to people, other animals, and a variety of common situations. You want to make an informed decision to ensure your new pet is a good fit for you, your family, and your lifestyle.

How much will it cost for food, supplies, accessories, and healthcare for your new pet?

Here is a list of potential expenses for the various pets in this book. This is *not* a comprehensive list of everything you would need for a specific pet.

- Adoption fee
- Spay or neutering (if not included in adoption fee)
- Vaccinations
- Flea treatment
- Licensing fees, permits
- ID Tags
- Microchip
- Pet Health Insurance
- Food or reliable food source
- Food & water bowls
- Bed

- Leash
- Collar
- Harness
- Toys
- Poop bags
- Nail clippers
- Litter box
- Litter
- Scoop
- Bath accessories: shampoo, comb, brush, towels
- Habitat supplies and equipment for a reptile
- Cage related supplies for a bird, rabbit, Guinea Pig or hamster
- Pet door
- Crate for use in the house
- Crate for carrying/transporting the animal

Will the added expense of owning a pet fit comfortably in your monthly budget? You can find the average yearly cost to maintain various pets on the Internet.

Example: Potential monthly expenses for a dog include:

- Food
- Dog Training
- Dog Grooming
- Doggie Daycare
- Flea treatment and or medication.

Additional funds may be needed to repair or replace a fence or gate, shoes, slippers, rugs, computer cords or for unexpected veterinarian care.

Whether you adopt an adolescent animal or a mature animal, it's a good idea to set aside extra money for at least the first few months to cover unexpected expenses. If something does happen, you'll be better prepared to deal with the added expense.

If you adopt an animal with health problems, be sure to include additional costs for medication, treatment, regular veterinarian checkups, or possibly a specialized caregiver in your monthly pet budget. If you place your pet in the care of a professional pet sitter or boarding facility, you'll likely pay extra if they need to give your pet medication or take it to the vet.

Popular Pets

Films, commercials, dog shows, holidays, and celebrities have all generated mass appeal for a specific breed or type of pet.

Dalmatians became very popular after the release of a Disney movie; people were suddenly crazy for Dalmatians and everyone had to have one! But, once their new Dalmatian puppy was home, they soon discovered it was an extremely active and energetic dog that needed a lot of attention and daily exercise. People were also surprised to find their cute little puppy would grow into a 70lb dog!

Teacup dogs became quite popular after a few celebrities began carrying their teacup-sized dog around with them. Teacup dogs tend to weigh 4 to 5 pounds or less; they are delicate little dogs and must be handled carefully.

Obviously, they can also be quite vulnerable to other animals, an important consideration if you want a teacup dog and you have other pets. You'll need to take care to keep your teacup dog warm in cool weather, and regular meals are absolutely necessary to maintain good health. They often experience more health challenges than larger dogs, so healthcare costs will likely be higher.

A teacup may seem like the perfect pet if your living quarters are tight. But such a small dog can be hard to keep track of, a door left ajar just a little can provide an opportunity to escape. There are many things to consider before you run out and adopt the same type of pet your favorite celebrity is toting around.

Easter is a good example of how a holiday can popularize a specific type of animal. Lots of "Easter Bunnies" are adopted for children every year, but rabbits are not necessarily the perfect pet for young children. Domesticated rabbits require a lot of care, attention, and maintenance. You can't expect a child to bear the burden of caring for a pet rabbit.

Exotic species are also vulnerable to fads, and sellers of these pets can be people trying to make a lot of money by selling the animals for excessively high prices. In many states, it's illegal to own certain types of exotic animals.

You may live in a state where exotic animals are permitted, but if you acquire one and you're unable or unwilling to keep the animal, re-homing it can be challenging. Your local Humane Society or animal shelter probably won't accept an exotic animal.

Exotic animals are not like domesticated pets, nor do they have the temperament of domesticated animals. They have specific habitat requirements and special dietary needs which you may *not* be able to meet. Exotic animals carry more disease than domestic animals. If the animal becomes ill, it may be difficult to find a veterinarian who is trained and/or willing to treat it.

So, the next time you see a super cute dog in a movie and think, "This is the dog for me!" Or your child begs you for an "Easter Bunny" (other than the chocolate variety) or asks for a pet Iguana—stop and think before you run to the nearest shelter or breeder.

Investigate, research, talk to a veterinarian, breeder, other owners, rescue organization or shelter about the pet you're contemplating adopting. Weigh the pros and cons before you promise the kid's they'll get a bunny in their Easter basket, or a dog like the one in their favorite movie.

A Pet for a Child

If you have a child, they have probably asked for a dog or cat, or talked about their friend's Guinea Pig and mentioned how fun it would be to have one of their own. Or, maybe they've brought home a stray dog or cat and pleaded with you to let them keep it. Animals and children can be great together. With your supervision and direction, caring for a pet will teach your child responsibility, compassion, respect, and love.

It's important to talk with your child about a pet *before* you bring one home. Of course, it can be fun to surprise your child with a new pet, but first make sure it's the right pet for your child and for your family. Find out why your child wants a pet? Do they want a dog to play fetch in the backyard or at the park? Or, would they like a small pet like a Guinea Pig or hamster they can keep in their bedroom? Or would they like to have a kitten because their friend has one and they want a kitten, too?

Your child also needs to understand the capabilities and limitations of the pet they want. If their expectations are unrealistic, you'll need to explain what they can realistically expect from the animal they want, and/or discuss other pets which could better meet their expectations.

You'll need to teach your child how and when to touch and handle their new pet. For example, dogs can be very protective of their food and may bite if they are touched while eating. Not all cats enjoy being be picked up, held or carried and may scratch or bite, especially if frightened. Rabbits have fragile spines and should to be picked up carefully and held gently to prevent injuries.

Consider your child's current commitments: school, homework, after-school and weekend activities, sports, clubs, etc. How much responsibility are they able to assume for a pet? Would they be responsible for a daily walk, play, feeding, grooming, yard clean up, cage cleaning?

Your child may agree to a variety of chores and responsibilities if they think it will help them acquire the pet they want. They may happily hold up their end of the bargain for the first week, two weeks or even a month. You need to be realistic about whether your child will follow through with their responsibilities regularly. If you're constantly reminding them to look after their pet, both you and they will feel frustrated. It's quite possible to end up resenting the pet—and the animal suffers.

If your child has asthma, allergies, or other health conditions consult with their physician before adopting a pet.

Communication Between You and Your Pet

We know good communication forms the basis of happy and fulfilling relationships with our human family. Good communication between you and your pet is also a vital part of developing a happy and healthy relationship.

There are lots of ways to communicate with your pet. Dogs and cats can learn words and they respond to body language and facial expressions. Your pet will also respond to the tone and pitch of your voice. And you may be surprised to learn some animals will respond to your intentions and the mental images you create which involve them.

You may not be aware of just how often you create images in your mind. Have you ever created the image of a parking space while on your way to a specific location? Or visualized a yummy dessert you were looking forward to enjoying on your birthday? Or maybe you have visualized something you were planning to do before you did it? Perhaps you imagined or created an image in your mind of someone you were going to meet and how they might look or be dressed?

Here's an example of intention and mental images communicated between a person and their dog. Janet tells her friend Sue she just took her new puppy to the vet for vaccinations. During their conversation, Sue remembers her dog Bailey needs his rabies vaccination. The next day Sue calls the vet and schedules an appointment for Bailey the following Monday.

Monday morning Sue takes Bailey for a walk before his appointment with the veterinarian. During their walk, Sue is watching Bailey, and remembers the last time she took him to the vet. Sue creates a mental image of Bailey not wanting to jump into the car before they left. It was as if he knew this car ride was different and he didn't want to go. Sue wonders if it's going to be difficult to get Bailey into the car this time?

Sue visualizes Dr. Wilson giving Bailey a shot and winces a little at the image in her mind. Next, she visualizes Bailey getting lots of at-a-boys and pets from Dr. Wilson, and Bailey looking at Dr. Wilson and wagging his tail.

Sue has just visualized part of a previous experience of taking Bailey to the vet, as well as visualizing his upcoming experience with the vet. Bailey has possibly picked up on Sue's intention and the mental images she created for his appointment with the vet today.

You can use intention and mental images when training your pet to learn a new behavior or change unwanted behaviors.

Example: Your dog greets visitors by jumping up on them when they enter your home.

If you've witnessed this behavior many times, you've probably developed a habit of creating a mental image or visualization of your dog jumping people when they walk into your home. Visualizing your dog's negative behavior simply reinforces the behavior.

In addition to training your dog to greet people politely when they enter your home, visualize your dog performing and following through with the new behavior he or she is learning.

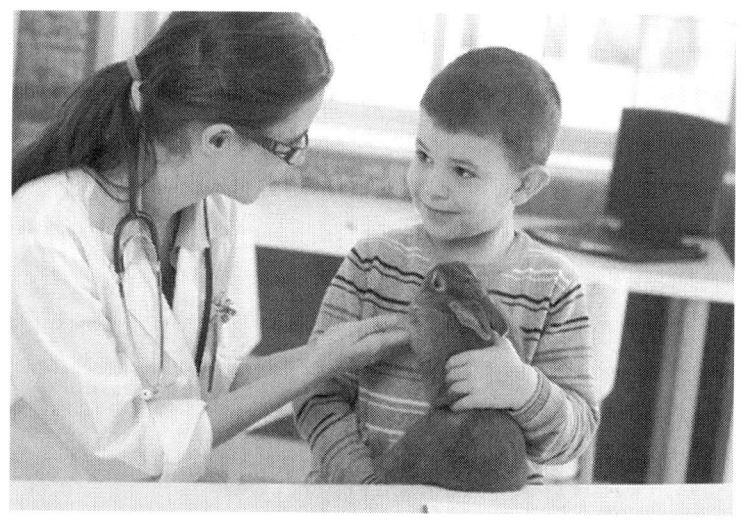

Illness

Health problems can be one of the most emotionally and financially challenging issues you'll ever face as a pet owner. Medication and treatment for an ill or injured pet can quickly skyrocket into hundreds, even thousands of dollars. Depending on the age and overall health of your pet, pet insurance could be an option to help offset the cost of healthcare.

If you're aware of your pet's normal eating and sleeping habits, potty routine, and activity level, changes which could indicate physical or emotional distress may be more noticeable.

A regular feeding schedule is important for your pets and will also help you recognize a shift or change in your pet's eating habits. Monitor your pet's weight—weight gain or loss may signal your pet is experiencing a health problem, or an issue with their diet.

Pets typically establish a routine of preferred times and places to sleep; a change in sleeping habits may be a sign your pet is not physically or emotionally comfortable. Grooming habits are also significant. If your pet suddenly stops grooming or begins pulling its hair out, he or she may be experiencing emotional stress, allergies, or other health issues.

An attentive pet owner will usually notice obvious signs of distress or illness in their pet, but illness is not always obvious or easy to spot. Cats are often very good at hiding pain and illness. Regular vet visits are an important part of proactive healthcare for your pet. A routine checkup can detect a health problem which has not yet revealed itself in an obvious manner.

A sick or injured pet will likely receive more of your time and attention than usual with trips to the veterinarian, receiving medication and/or care for a wound, etc. But this kind of attention probably won't fulfill your pet's need for connection and interaction with you.

If your pet is unable to go for walks, run or play, you'll need to find other ways to spend quality time together. Enjoying time together that doesn't focus on a health issue or injury is important for your pet's physical and emotional healing and well-being.

If your pet is experiencing a chronic condition, you may want to talk to your veterinarian about alternative therapies which could accompany traditional medication and treatment. Alternative therapies include acupuncture, acupressure, homeopathy, chiropractic, massage, and herbal remedies.

A new person moving into the home you share with a pet

When a new person moves into your home there will likely be an adjustment phase for your pet. If the new person and your pet are already acquainted and have previously established a good relationship, the transition will likely be smooth. If the new person and your pet have not met or have only met on a few occasions, your pet will need time to become accustomed to the sound of the new person's voice, their appearance, smell, habits, and interaction with you.

Consider the new person's lifestyle, style of dress, and any behaviors which may be foreign to your pet. A person using a cane, walker, or wheelchair may scare some animals. A person wearing a hat may frighten some dogs, an electric razor will likely scare a cat. Loud noises, voices, music, or TV, could also cause your pet to feel stressed if this is out of the norm.

Animals are similar to people in that they become quite attached to their routine. If it's necessary to change your pet's routine to accommodate a new member of the household, do so slowly and ease your pet into the new schedule.

Pets can be quite possessive of their person or people. A friend or roommate moving into your home may only be a mild adjustment for your pet, but a new spouse or partner (or child) can be more challenging. Your pet may feel a little jealous and act out if a new spouse or partner infringes on time you usually spend together.

A dog can be quite protective of their people and their environment. A new person moving into your home could trigger your dog's instinct to defend and protect you and your home.

How the new person responds to and interacts with your pet will also influence the adjustment phase. Is the new person comfortable and at ease with your pet? Are they interested in creating a relationship with your pet? Do they attempt to interact with your pet? If they are not familiar with your pet or the type of animal you have, it's essential for you to demonstrate how to interact with your pet.

If your new housemate is genuinely interested in cultivating a relationship with your pet, have them assist you when you feed your pet, or go with you when you walk your pet. Gradually include the new person in play time and games your pet enjoys; let them throw the ball, Frisbee, or toy mouse.

Pay attention to your pet's behavior when your new housemate is home, does your pet seem comfortable and at ease, or uncomfortable and tense? Notice if your pet attempts to be close and/or spend time with the new person, or if they avoid an opportunity to interact.

How does your pet act when the new housemate is away? When they come home does your pet seem happy, excited, interested to see them, or fearful and stressed? Is your pet behaving in a way that is not normal when you prepare to leave, and your new housemate is home? Is your pet's behavior unusual when you return home?

The following are signals that your pet is feeling scared, threatened, or jealous: excessive barking, whining or meowing; hiding, growling, biting, screeching, hissing, swatting, scratching, pulling their fur out or other stress response. Your pet may also exhibit reduced activity, depression, loss of appetite, diarrhea, freezing in place, tail tucked, trying to escape. Your pet may demonstrate destructive or aggressive behavior, urinating or defecating around the house (or specifically on the new person's property).

If your pet is exhibiting any of the behaviors listed above, you'll first need to ascertain if your new housemate is intentionally doing anything to provoke, anger, scare or hurt your pet. If you find they are abusing the animal in any way, they need to move out immediately!

If you've ruled out the previously mentioned issues and your pet still seems uncomfortable with the new person, your veterinarian, a certified animal behaviorist or animal communicator may be able to discover what is troubling your pet.

Animals are not necessarily as selective as people when it comes to those they like and dislike, but animals do feel at ease with some people and uncomfortable or threatened by others. *You cannot force your pet to like or engage with anyone.*

A new person moving into your home will *not* need an agreement with your pet. Even if they cultivate a relationship with your pet, the agreement is only between you and your pet.

Miscommunication Between You and Your Pet

Misunderstandings will happen between you and your pet, and probably more often when you're feeling angry or frustrated with something your pet is doing.

Sometimes animals combine a behavior you want with one you don't want. It can be challenging to figure out how to communicate to your pet which behavior you want changed.

My friend Cynthia had just such a problem with her cat, Beth. Every morning as Cynthia was waking up, Beth would come into her bedroom, jump up on the bed and cuddle with her. Cynthia loved this special time she shared with Beth. The problem was Beth occasionally liked to stretch and dig her claws into the bedspread a few times before she jumped up onto the bed.

Beth had a scratching post, which she used; and she didn't claw the furniture, but for some reason the bedspread seemed to be irresistible to her. Cynthia didn't know what to do to stop Beth from clawing the bedspread.

One morning as Beth stretched and began digging her claws into the bedspread, Cynthia yelled at her and Beth ran out of the bedroom. The next two mornings Beth didn't come into Cynthia's bedroom. It seemed Beth didn't understand why Cynthia had yelled at her.

Cynthia felt bad about losing her temper and yelling at Beth, and she certainly didn't want Beth to stop cuddling with her in the morning. She also felt frustrated because she didn't know how to communicate to Beth the type of behavior she wanted and which she didn't.

Animals are creatures of habit, which can work in both positive and negative ways. Fortunately, with a little coaxing, soon Beth was back to her normal routine of coming into the bedroom in the morning and jumping up onto the bed to cuddle. Cynthia was happy Beth had resumed her morning routine, but she knew the problem was not resolved. It was just a matter of time before Beth would once again sink her claws into the bedspread.

Cynthia just didn't know what to do to separate the two behaviors. How could she stop Beth from digging her claws into the bedspread before she jumped up onto the bed? Obviously, Beth had the two behaviors connected even if she didn't do both all the time.

The easy way to solve the problem was to remove the bedspread or put something over the bedspread which would protect it from Beth's claws. But Cynthia first wanted to see if she could change Beth's behavior.

I suggested Cynthia set the intention for the behavior she wanted and visualize Beth coming into the bedroom in the morning and jumping up onto the bed without pausing to dig her claws into the bedspread. If Beth did pause and go after the bedspread, Cynthia could gently push Beth's paws away from the bedspread and say "No" firmly, but without yelling. Then she could invite Beth up onto the bed.

Cynthia began to visualize Beth jumping up onto the bed without pausing to claw the bedspread. It took a little time for Beth to understand what Cynthia wanted from her, but eventually Beth ceased digging her claws into the bedspread and began to jump right up onto the bed to share a morning cuddle.

An Agreement Between You and Your Pet

Writing an agreement for a pet you're planning to adopt

The example agreements in this book are designed to encourage you to think about your reasons for adopting a pet, and the relationship you hope to have with your pet. What do you want and expect from a pet? What are you willing and able to do for your pet? How will you deal with changes and problems that may arise between you and your pet?

Start by reading the example agreement that pertains to the type of pet you intend to adopt.

Following the example agreement, begin your own agreement by writing about your reasons for adopting a pet, and the purpose it will fulfill in your life.

Example: "I want to adopt a dog for companionship. I want my dog to accompany me on daily walks. Walking my dog around my neighborhood will be a lot more fun and interesting than walking on my treadmill. I think walking a dog will also be kind of an ice breaker, and make it easier for me to meet my neighbors."

In the example above the person could visualize walking his dog around the neighborhood and meeting his neighbors. He could also visualize other activities and experiences he looks forward to having with his dog.

Follow the example agreement and list the behaviors, lifestyle, and activities you would like your pet to learn, accept, and tolerate.

The agreement should not include behaviors, a lifestyle, activities, or a job which can cause the animal physical, mental, or emotional harm.

All relationships require give and take on both sides to maintain balance and harmony. Maybe you want your dog to learn basic obedience commands: come, sit, stay, heel, leave it, lie down. It is your responsibility to take the time to teach your dog the commands. If you choose not to teach the commands yourself, you have the option of obedience training classes.

Maybe you're planning to adopt a bird with a reputation for mimicking speech, with the hope it will learn words, phrases, or songs. You must be willing to devote the time, energy, and patience necessary to teach your bird to talk or sing. The caveat is some birds—even those with a reputation for talking—may *never* learn to talk. Are you willing to accept the bird you adopt may never talk, regardless of your efforts?

If you expect your pet bird to accept living in a cage, you should be willing to provide your bird with an appropriately sized cage, outfit the cage with everything your pet bird needs and spend time interacting with it daily.

Maybe you're planning to adopt a cat and you want your pet to accept living as an indoor pet. Your cat needs daily interaction and to play with you and your family members. Cats sleep a lot, but they also need regular exercise and mental stimulation.

A cat tree can provide play and exercise for your indoor cat. A window seat or hammock for cats gives your cat a comfy place to sleep and watch what's happening outside. (Make sure the window and screen are safe and secure, especially for a second-story window or higher.)

As you write this part of the agreement, you are setting your intention for what you want from your pet. Remember to visualize the behaviors, lifestyle, and activities you would like your pet to learn, accept, or tolerate.

It may take up to a year or longer for a new pet to become comfortable with you, family members, and its environment. Keep this in mind as you list the behaviors, lifestyle, activities or a job you would like your pet to learn, accept, or tolerate.

An agreement does not guarantee your pet will learn, accept, or tolerate, a behavior, lifestyle, activity, or job.

Follow the example agreement and list your responsibilities.

I am willing and able to provide the following for my pet

Include everything you are willing and able to provide and do for your pet. Here are some examples:

► Attention, play, exercise, training classes

► A safe home environment

► A proper diet, and regular feeding schedule, fresh water

► An adequately sized crate, hutch, cage, or enclosure

► Healthcare

► Regular grooming or bathing

► Having someone to care for your pet when you're away, etc.

► Keep in mind your pet will be fully dependent on you for its care and well-being.

As you write this part of the agreement, visualize yourself performing the tasks you've listed as well as giving your pet attention and playing together. If you're writing an agreement for a dog, visualize yourself teaching your dog basic obedience commands, or attending obedience training classes.

If you're planning to adopt a dog and you would like it to learn a job, follow the example agreement

A job for my dog

When you write this part of the agreement for a dog you intend to adopt, you need to keep in mind the job you would like your dog to learn may or may not be a match for the dog you ultimately bring home. Update the agreement as necessary.

Dogs have been bred for specific jobs ever since people began domesticating their wolf ancestors. Most dogs are excited to have a job that gives them the opportunity to express their natural skills and abilities. For certain breeds, a job is necessary for both exercise and mental stimulation.

If you adopt a dog from a shelter, you'll likely adopt a mixed breed. The shelter will probably be able to give you some idea of the breed which seems to be the most dominant in the dog you are considering adopting.

Educate yourself about your potential dog's dominant breed and about the specific job this breed was originally bred to do. This can be useful information when contemplating a job for your dog. Also consider the dog's purpose in your life, his or her age, size, temperament, mental and emotional maturity, physical ability, training, and history.

Instincts are helpful, but your dog will need training, guidance, and direction to learn a job. *Never correct or discipline your dog with physical punishment or yelling.* If you're having difficulty training your dog, hire a professional dog trainer; they will show you how to work with your dog.

Example: "My hearing is not what it used to be, and I don't always hear the phone when someone calls or when I get a text message. I would like my dog to learn to alert me when someone calls or sends a text."

As you write this part of the agreement, remember to visualize your dog performing the job you would like him or her to learn.

Follow the example agreement and list reasons why you would need to update the agreement

Over the course of your life together, you will need to update the agreement. If there is something in the agreement your pet is unwilling or unable to do, accept or tolerate, remove it from the agreement.

Example: "I want my dog's job to be going to work with me." Then you discover every time your dog goes for a ride in the car, he gets carsick. If you don't want to continue cleaning up after your pet each time you bring him to work with you in your car, you may want to remove this job from your *Agreement*.

Example: Your pet now requires daily medication. In the appropriate place in your Agreement, you now need to include the words, "I will provide the medication my pet needs daily."

Writing an agreement between you and your future pet is a positive step you can take toward building a happy, balanced, and healthy relationship. However, writing the agreement for a pet you intend to adopt does not guarantee the animal you do adopt will be a perfect fit for you and your family. Nor does it ensure you and your family will be a perfect fit for the animal.

When you bring your new pet home

Once you have your new pet home read over the agreement you created for you and your pet. Make any necessary changes or adjustments to the agreement. Here are a few things to be aware of and look for once your new pet is living with you.

If you already have a pet, pay close attention to how he or she is reacting to and interacting with the new pet. Is she trying to harm the new pet, or is the new pet trying to harm her? You can't expect or force your current pet to accept the new pet, nor can you expect or force the new pet to accept your current pet. Each animal must be willing to accept the other and cohabitate peacefully.

Observe how the new pet interacts with you and family members, and how family members interact with the new pet. Is anyone in your family experiencing allergies related to the new pet?

Is the new pet adjusting to you and your family? This is especially important if you have a baby, or small children, as not all animals are comfortable with children. It is your responsibility to make sure the interaction is safe and positive for both the child and the pet.

Is the new pet adjusting to the life you're providing for it? Is he or she comfortable inside your home and outside—if they spend time outside? Is your pet eating, sleeping, grooming, and getting into a regular routine? Is she getting enough play, exercise, and interaction with you and family members?

Everyone in the family (people and pets) will need time to adjust to each other, and your new pet will need time to become comfortable with his or her new family and life.

Within about four weeks you'll probably have some indication of how things are working between you, family members and your new pet. *It may take up to a year or longer for your pet to become comfortable with you, family members, and its environment. Keep this in mind regarding the lifestyle, behaviors, activities or a job you would like your pet to learn, accept, or tolerate.*

Writing an agreement between you and a pet you already have

Writing an agreement between you and your current pet is one way to support the positive behaviors your pet has already learned, and to set the intention for new behaviors you would like your pet to learn.

Start with the example agreement that pertains to the type of pet you have. Then, following the example agreement, begin your agreement by writing about how and why you got your pet. Also, write about the purpose he or she fulfills in your life.

Example: "For my ninth birthday my mom and dad surprised me with a silver tabby kitten. He was an awesome cat and he was still with us when I left home for University. I missed him so much when I was away at school, and I loved seeing him when I was home during holidays. He passed away a few months before I graduated, and I promised myself as soon as I got a job and settled in my new place, I would adopt a kitten."

"A year ago, I adopted a black and white tuxedo cat and named him Jackson. I'm so happy to have him, he greets me at the door purring and meowing when I come home from work. I enjoy my job, but it's stressful, so after a long day at work I spend time with Jackson and the stress just goes away."

Follow the example agreement and list the behaviors, lifestyle, and activities your pet has learned, accepts, and tolerates

When you have finished listing the behaviors, lifestyle, and activities your pet has already learned, add any new behaviors or activities you would like your pet to learn. As you write this part of the agreement you are setting your intention for what you want from your pet. Remember to visualize your pet performing new behaviors or activities.

The agreement should not include behaviors, a lifestyle, activities or a job which cause the animal physical, mental, or emotional harm.

Follow the example agreement and list your responsibilities

"I am willing and able to provide the following for my pet..."

You are likely already fulfilling many of the responsibilities listed in the example agreement. List your current responsibilities and add any new responsibilities you're willing to assume for your pet. As you write this part of the agreement, visualize yourself performing any new tasks you've added to the list.

If you have a dog and you would like him to learn a job, follow the example agreement

A job for my dog

Dogs have been bred for specific jobs ever since people began domesticating their wolf ancestors. Most dogs are excited to have a job that gives them the opportunity to express their natural skills and abilities. For certain breeds, a job is necessary for both exercise and mental stimulation.

If you have adopted a mixed breed, you probably have some knowledge of the breed that is the most dominant. Educate yourself about the dominant breed and the specific job it was originally bred to do. This can be useful information when contemplating a job for your dog. Also, consider your dog's purpose in your life, its age, size, temperament, mental and emotional maturity, physical ability, training, and history.

Instincts are helpful, but your dog will need training, guidance, and direction to learn a job. *Never correct or discipline your dog with physical punishment or yelling.* If you're having difficulty training your dog, hire a professional dog trainer, they will show you how to work with your dog.

Example: "I own a small business and I would like my dog to go to work with me. She likes people and she's very friendly. She'll have lots of attention when she wants it and I'll create a comfortable space for her with food, water, toys, and a bed for when she wants to sleep or relax."

As you write this part of the agreement, remember to visualize your dog performing the job you would like her to learn.

Follow the example agreement and list reasons why you would need to update the agreement

Over the course of your life together, you will need to update the agreement. If there is something in the agreement your pet is unwilling or unable to do, accept, or tolerate, remove it from the agreement.

Example: Your pet now requires daily medication. Under the section "I am willing and able to give my pet _____." Include the name or a description of the medication it needs daily.

An agreement does not guarantee your pet will learn, accept, or tolerate a behavior, lifestyle, activity, or job.

Emergency or Natural Disaster

It's essential to have an evacuation kit for yourself *and* for your pet. Your pet's evacuation kit should include all the items it needs to survive for at least seventy-two hours, but seven days is optimum.

Here's a list of *some* items you may need in your pet's evacuation kit:

► A travel carrier for each of your pets with your pets name (your name and your contact information should be on the carrier)

► A leash, harness, collar, and tag with your pet's name and your contact information

► Bottled water, food—canned and dry food if your pet normally eats both, as well as treats

► Bowls for food and water, a can opener, a spoon, paper towels, baby wipes, disposable bags to clean up after your pet

► Cage liners, disposable litter trays, extra litter, and a scoop

► A toy and familiar blanket or towel— one that smells like you or home

- First-aid kit and any medication your pet requires (make a note to rotate food and medications in your pet's evacuation kit to keep them fresh)

- Current medical and vaccination records

- Add a photo of you and your pet together.

This is not a complete list of everything you may need in your pet's evacuation kit; be sure to stock the kit with everything your pet requires.

Your pet's evacuation kit is also useful in the event of a natural disaster or other situation which creates the need for you and your pet to shelter-in-place. If you must confine yourself and your pet to one room, you'll have everything your pet needs with you.

Legal Documents Involving Your Pet

As a responsible pet owner, it's important for you to have a plan ensuring your pet will be well cared for in the event of your passing. A pet trust is one way to leave money for the care of your pet. Talk to the person you would like to be trustee of the pet trust and make sure they are willing to accept responsibility for managing money in the trust.

Most people have heard of a prenuptial agreement, a legally binding document created to protect property in the event of divorce. A "pet-nup" is similar to a prenup but it covers what happens to a pet in a divorce.

Legally pets are considered personal property. If you and your partner are unable to come to an agreement regarding the custody and care for your pet, a judge can decide what happens to the pet.

In the case of shared custody, a pet-nup can also cover how each person should care for the pet, dog training classes, grooming, breeding, who pays for what, etc.

Living Agreements

Living agreements are beliefs, attitudes, and habits which influence our choice of pet, our expectations of a pet, and ultimately the relationship we have with our pet. The roots of living agreements are found in childhood experiences with pets, our family's attitude about pets, what society tells us to think and feel about pets, and observing people interacting with their pets.

We generally don't question our living agreements, nor do we consider them from the animal's point of view. We expect our pet will simply understand and respond accordingly.

Some of us identify so much with our pet we almost feel it is an extension of ourselves, so when we feel disconnected with or have a misunderstanding with our pet, we may become confused and frustrated. But we are different—for all our similarities—and how we each express love is one of the ways. Keep this in mind as you consider your own living agreements.

Human beings have the ability to love their pet from a distance, but for the most part, animals love up close. What does this mean? Our pets want to be physically close to us, dogs and cats especially. An animal's attempt to be close and loving is often interpreted as bad behavior, because the person doesn't understand the intention motivating the behavior.

Here are some examples of living agreements:

"I expect my dog to quietly and patiently wait for me to return home from work each day. She should not bark, chew on my shoes, or get on the furniture."

Example: A person goes to work and they are gone for many hours. While they are gone, their dog looks for them and finds their clothes or shoes. The dog chews on the person's clothes or shoes in an effort to be close to the person.

The person comes home from work, finds the chewed clothes or shoes, becomes angry, and yells at the dog. The dog, however, is happy and excited to see the person after a long day alone and doesn't understand why the person is angry and yelling.

This scenario plays out over, and over again, with the person coming home after a long absence, getting angry and yelling at the dog. Eventually, the dog doesn't know how to be close or love the person.

"I put my dog in the backyard in the morning before I go to work, and I expect him to stay there until I get home from work."

Example: A dog is left alone and unleashed in the backyard. The person goes to work in the morning and is gone all day. At some point during the day, the dog becomes bored, lonely, or frightened, digs a hole under the fence, and escapes out of the backyard. The person comes home from work and becomes angry when they find their dog dug a hole under the fence and is no longer in the backyard.

When the person finally finds the dog running around the neighborhood, they grab the dog and yell, "Bad dog!" over, and over again. The dog is happy and excited to finally see his or her person, and doesn't understand why they are angry and yelling.

As in the above example, this scenario plays out over, and over. Eventually, the dog doesn't know how to be close to or love the person.

"My rabbit has plenty of things to chew on in her cage. She shouldn't need to chew on computer cords, baseboards, or anything else in the house when I let her out."

Example: A person lets their rabbit out of its cage so it can stretch, run around, and get some exercise. The doorbell rings and the person leaves the rabbit for a few minutes to answer the door.

When the person returns, they find the rabbit chewing on computer cords. They suddenly become angry and shout at the rabbit. The rabbit doesn't understand why the person is angry and shouting. The rabbit always seems to find something to chew on when it is out of its cage, and the person always yells and becomes angry.

Eventually, the rabbit doesn't want to come out of its cage or be close to the person. The person doesn't understand why the rabbit seems frightened when it's out of its cage.

"I've heard cats can be picky about their food, but the cat we had when I was a kid was happy to eat whatever food we gave him. I expect my cat to be like him and eat the food I give her."

Example: A person has been feeding their cat a specific type of food for a while; suddenly the cat stops eating the food. The person goes to the store and buys a different flavor of food, hoping the cat will eat it. The cat sniffs the new food and walks away. Frustrated but persistent, the person tries another brand or flavor.

This time the cat eats the food and the person is happy—the problem is solved. The next day, or maybe a week or two later, the person gives the cat the same food but now the cat won't eat it. The person feels frustrated the cat is so picky about its food.

This scenario plays out over-and-over again and the person becomes increasingly frustrated and annoyed each time the cat won't eat the food. The cat senses the person's anger and begins to feel fearful about food, eating, *and* the person at mealtime. The cat doesn't understand why the person is angry when offering food.

Here are some more examples of living agreements:

"I expect my cat to use the litter box even if I only get around to cleaning it once or twice a week."

"My dog is aggressive toward other dogs, but when I adopt another dog, I expect it to be friendly towards and accept the new dog."

"The cat I adopted has always been an outdoor cat, but I expect he will get used to living as an indoor cat."

"I loved the way my grandmother's parakeet talked and sang. I just adopted a parakeet and I expect it to learn to talk and sing like my grandmother's parakeet."

"I expect my cat to be friendly toward people who come into our home."

"I expect the rabbit I adopted to be a good pet for my children."

Agreements and Love

You will probably notice the word "love" is not included in any of the example agreements in this book. I expect if you are planning to adopt a pet—and certainly if you're reading this book—you have or are hoping to have a loving bond between you and your pet.

We all want to experience feelings of love/affection/loyalty in our relationships. Each of us recognizes and experiences these feelings in our own way, so it's difficult to include a description in an agreement.

Love can be an expression of a feeling, an emotion, a manifestation of loyalty, an expression of affection, and much more. So, let's agree to leave these words out of the agreement between ourselves and our pets, and trust that the feelings these words represent will be part of the relationships we build with the pets who are part of our lives.

Love, affection, and loyalty are not the same as committing to take your pet to the veterinarian when it's not well, or agreeing to clean your Guinea Pig's cage, or agreeing to feed your pet rabbit a healthy diet.

Therefore, I have not included feelings of love/affection/loyalty in the agreements. I have simply referred to comfort and physical care, nurturing, responsibilities, activities, training—things you can see, measure, and do.

It's certainly a good thing to realize that "Love" is not a job, or a responsibility, or a chore. Love is a feeling, an emotion, an expression of affection, and as such "Love" cannot be contractual. Let's leave the word "love" out of our agreements and trust love itself will be a part of our relationship with our pet.

A Dog for Companionship

Are you planning to adopt a puppy or an adult dog? A puppy will require a significant amount of your time, energy, and patience.

Be prepared to make some adjustments in your home environment to accommodate your new puppy or dog. Dogs like to chew so cords, wires, small toys, shoes, and plants, among other things, should be out of reach. You can use childproof locks to keep your dog out of cabinets containing food, cleaning products, medications, and garbage.

Do you have a secure yard or outdoor space to walk and exercise a dog?

If you have asthma, allergies, or other health conditions, consult with your physician before adopting a dog.

Suggestions for an agreement between you and your companion dog

Example: *Why I want a dog for companionship.*

"I live alone, sometimes I feel lonely. I think a dog will ease the loneliness of coming home from work to an empty house. I look forward to my dog greeting me with a bark and wagging his tail when I get home. We can go for walks in the neighborhood and the park. I'll take my dog on vacation with me. I can't wait for us to get together with my friends and their dogs."

The agreement should not include behaviors, a lifestyle, activities or a job which cause the animal physical, mental, or emotional harm.

Visualize the behaviors and activities you would like your dog to learn, accept, or tolerate, as you write the agreement.

I want my dog to

- Participate in obedience training classes
- Learn to respond to commands
- Learn to communicate the need for food and attention
- Learn to communicate fear
- Learn to play fetch and Frisbee
- Learn to walk on-leash
- Learn its name
- Tolerate physical examination from a veterinarian
- Tolerate grooming: bath, haircut, brushing, nails trimmed
- Tolerate cleaning and care of teeth and ears
- Tolerate sleeping in a crate. (*Consult a professional dog trainer for information and advice regarding the correct way to crate-train your dog.*)

It may take up to a year or longer for your dog to become comfortable with you and its environment. Keep this in mind as you list the behaviors, lifestyle, activities or job you would like your dog to learn, accept or tolerate.

I am willing and able to provide the following for my dog

- Attention
- A safe and secure home environment

- A routine and regular feeding schedule; fresh water to drink
- A diet which meets my dog's physical needs and requirements
- The exercise my dog needs daily
- Obedience training classes (and practice sessions)
- Healthcare, regular physical exams from a veterinarian
- An appropriately sized crate
- Competent care when I'm away from home for an extende+d period: a pet sitter, or boarding kennel
- Prearranged care for my dog in the event I'm unable to care for him/her

A job for my dog

The dog you ultimately adopt will be an important factor in this part of the agreement. A puppy will need socialization, obedience training, time to grow, mature, and bond with you before learning a job. An adult dog will also need training and time to bond with you before learning a job.

When considering a job for your dog think about the dog's purpose in your life as well as its age, size, breed, natural skills and abilities, temperament, mental and emotional maturity, physical ability, training, and history.

Here's a short list of potential jobs for a companion dog

- Be close to me when I am relaxing, reading, watching TV, working on the computer
- Bark when someone knocks on the door or rings the doorbell
- Pick up its toys
- Accompany me when I exercise: daily walks, running, hiking
- Go to work with me.

Instincts are helpful, but your dog will need training, guidance, and direction to learn a job. *Never correct or discipline your dog with physical punishment or yelling.* If you're having difficulty training your dog, hire a professional dog trainer, they will show you how to work with your dog.

Update your agreement

Over the course of your life together, you will need to update the agreement. If there is something in the agreement your dog is unwilling or unable to do, accept or tolerate, remove it from the agreement.

- ▶ Update the agreement when your dog takes on a job (Describe the job.)

- ▶ Update the agreement if there's a change to your dog's job description

- ▶ Update the agreement if your dog stops performing a job

- ▶ Update the agreement if there's a change in your dog's health. (Example: Your dog now requires daily medication. Under the section "I am willing and able to give my dog _____." Include the name or description of the medication it needs daily.)

Tip: Keep the agreement with your dog's veterinary records. At least once a year when you take your dog to the veterinarian for an annual exam, review the agreement and update as needed.

An agreement does not guarantee your pet will learn, accept, or tolerate a behavior, lifestyle, activity or job.

An agreement does not guarantee the pet you adopt will be a perfect fit for you.

Problems between you and your dog

"My dog and I come together for the fulfillment of mutual need. If I feel our relationship is not happy, I will adjust our agreement, focusing on the areas which pertain to the problems or challenges we are experiencing."

Note: Your veterinarian, a professional dog trainer, certified dog behaviorist, or animal communicator may be able to help you and your dog through a difficult time or situation.

"In the event happiness cannot be restored, I understand it is my responsibility to find a new guardian and a safe and suitable living arrangement for my dog."

Note: Surrendering your dog to a shelter, rescue organization, or new owner will end your agreement.

A Cat for Companionship

Are you planning to adopt a kitten or an adult cat? A kitten will require a significant amount of your time, energy, and patience. An adult cat will need some time to feel "at home" with you and in its new home.

Be prepared to make some adjustments in your home environment to accommodate your new kitten or cat. Cords and pulls attached to window coverings should be out of reach and never left hanging. Pick up small items which could be ingested: string, twist-ties, puzzle pieces, buttons.

Remove poisonous plants. You can use childproof locks to keep your cat out of cabinets containing food, cleaning products, medications, plastic bags, and garbage.

Whether you adopt a cat or kitten, it's a good idea to purchase a scratching post, cat tree, or climbing tower *before* you bring your new cat home. Scratching is an instinctive behavior for cats, they scratch to mark territory, stretch, express emotion, etc. In the *"Questions and Answers"* section, you'll find tips and steps you can take to encourage your cat to use a scratching post or cat tree.

Litter box placement is also an important consideration. I've seen litter boxes in some interesting places: bathtubs, bathroom cupboards, closets, etc. If you put the litter box in a cupboard or closet, you'll need to keep the door open, or cut a hole in the door. A dog can be trained to let you know when it needs to go out, but you likely won't be able to train your cat to let you know when it needs to go outside or use the litter box.

If you have asthma, allergies or other health conditions consult with your physician before adopting a cat.

Suggestions for an agreement between you and your companion cat

Example: *Why I want a cat for companionship.*

"I want a cat to keep me company. I'm not physically able to go for walks and the apartment where I live doesn't have any outdoor space. I love cats and I'm able to get around enough to play with a cat in the apartment."

"I have a few big windows in my apartment, I'll put a cat tree next to one of them so the cat can see outside and watch the birds. I can just imagine how nice it will be to have my cat sleeping on the bed with me at night and lying on my lap when I'm at the computer."

The agreement should not include behaviors, a lifestyle or activities which cause the animal physical, mental or emotional harm.

Visualize the behaviors and activities you would like your cat to learn, accept, and tolerate as you write the agreement.

I want my cat to

- ▶ Let me care for it

- ▶ Learn to use a scratching post or cat tree (The cat may still scratch furniture, rugs and/or carpet.)

- ▶ Learn to communicate the need for food and attention

- ▶ Learn to communicate fear

- ▶ Learn its name

- ▶ Learn interactive play

- ▶ Tolerate physical examination from a veterinarian (A visit to the vet can be extremely stressful for some cats. Talk to your veterinarian about how to handle a scared cat.)

- Tolerate being groomed: brushed, nails trimmed. (Some cats will not tolerate being groomed and some enjoy a bath or having their fur trimmed.)

- Tolerate being an indoor cat. (If you desire an indoor cat.)

- Tolerate being admired.

It may take up to a year or longer for your cat to become comfortable with you and its environment. Keep this in mind as you list the behaviors, lifestyle, and activities you would like your cat to learn, accept or tolerate.

I am willing and able to provide the following for my cat

- A safe and secure home environment

- Attention

- A regular routine and feeding schedule; a bowl of fresh water

- A diet which meets my cat's physical needs and requirements

- The play and exercise my cat needs daily (Cats need exercise, especially when they are young.)

- Access to a litter box which I clean daily

- Healthcare, regular physical exams from a veterinarian

- Competent care when I'm away from home for an extended period: a pet sitter, or boarding kennel

- Prearranged care for my cat in the event I'm unable to care for it.

Update your agreement

Over the course of your life together, you may need to update the agreement. If there is something in the agreement your cat is unwilling or unable to do, accept or tolerate, remove it from the agreement.

Update the agreement if there's a change in your cat's health. (*Example: Your cat now requires daily medication. Under the section "I am willing and able to give my cat _____." Include the name or description of the medication it needs daily.*)

Tip: Keep the agreement with your cat's veterinary records. At least once a year, when you take your cat to the veterinarian for an annual exam, review the agreement and update as needed.

An agreement does not guarantee your pet will learn, accept or tolerate a behavior, lifestyle or activity.

An agreement does not guarantee the pet you adopt will be a perfect fit for you.

Problems between you and your cat

"My cat and I come together for the fulfillment of mutual need. If I feel our relationship is not happy, I will adjust our agreement, focusing on the areas which pertain to the problems or challenges we are experiencing."

Note: Your veterinarian, a certified cat behaviorist, or animal communicator may be able to help you and your cat through a difficult time or situation.

"In the event happiness cannot be restored, I understand it is my responsibility to find a new guardian and a safe and suitable living arrangement for my cat."

Note: Surrendering your cat to a shelter, rescue organization, or new owner will end your agreement.

A Bird for Companionship

There are many things to consider before you adopt a pet bird: species, size, lifespan (which can be quite long for some birds), daily care, etc. In the *"More Information About the Pets in This Book"* section, you'll find information about size and lifespan for some of the most common pet birds.

Be prepared to make some adjustments in your home environment to accommodate your new bird. Most birds require time out of their cage daily for play and exercise.

Here are a few precautions you can take to help ensure your bird's safety:

- ▶ Cover windows and sliding doors so the bird doesn't fly into the glass

- ▶ Cords and pulls attached to window coverings should not be left hanging

- ▶ Turn ceiling fans off

- ▶ Cover cooling and heating air ducts

If you hope to train your bird to talk, ask the breeder if the breeding pair had been trained to talk. Note: *Some birds simply can't be trained to talk. Don't adopt a bird and assume it will learn to talk or sing.*

Do you live in a detached house, apartment, or condo? Certain species can be quite loud; you may enjoy the sound of your bird's voice, but can you say the same for you neighbors?

Feather dust can aggravate asthma in some people. If you or anyone living with you have asthma, allergies, or other health conditions, consult with your physician before adopting a bird.

Suggestions for an agreement between you and your companion bird

Example: *Why I want a bird for companionship.*

"My husband of 45 years passed a few years ago. I've felt very lonely without him and I think a pet will help fill the void. My good friend Debbie has two parakeets and I've come to love the little birds. I've spent a lot of time with her birds and have taken care of them when she's been out of town."

"It would be fun if my birds learn a few words but I'm okay if they don't. I'm so excited! I have the perfect space for the bird cage, and the company of my pet birds will bring me a lot of pleasure and comfort."

The agreement should not include behaviors, a lifestyle, or activities which cause the animal physical, mental, or emotional harm.

Visualize the behaviors and activities you would like your bird to learn, accept, and tolerate as you write the agreement.

I want my bird to

- ▶ Let me care for them
- ▶ Learn to communicate the need for food and attention
- ▶ Learn to communicate fear
- ▶ Learn to be sociable with people (It is your responsibility to socialize your bird.)
- ▶ Tolerate living in a cage
- ▶ Tolerate physical examination from a veterinarian
- ▶ Tolerate being groomed; nails trimmed, and wings clipped

▶ Tolerate being admired

It may take up to a year or longer for your bird to become comfortable with you and its environment. Keep this in mind as you list the behaviors, lifestyle or activities you would like your bird to learn, accept, or tolerate.

I am willing and able to provide the following for my bird

▶ Attention

▶ A safe and secure home environment

▶ An appropriately sized cage

▶ A regular routine and feeding schedule, fresh water

▶ A diet which meets my bird's physical needs and requirements

▶ Time out of their cage daily for play and exercise

▶ Regular opportunities for a bath

▶ A structure for climbing

▶ A clean cage (Daily cleaning)

▶ Adequate light exposure daily (Sunlight or specialized lighting)

▶ Healthcare, regular physical exams from a veterinarian

▶ Competent care when I'm away from home for an extended period: a pet sitter, or boarding kennel (Check availability in your area.)

▶ Prearranged care for my bird in the event I'm unable to care for it.

Update your agreement

Over the course of your life together, you may need to update the agreement. If there is something in the agreement your bird is unwilling or unable to do, accept or tolerate, remove it from the agreement.

Update the agreement if there's a change in your bird's health. (*Example: Your bird now requires daily medication. Under the section "I am willing and able to give my bird:_____." Include the name or description of the medication it needs daily.*)

Tip: Keep the agreement with your bird's veterinary records. At least once a year when you take your bird to the veterinarian for an annual exam, review the agreement and update as needed.

An agreement does not guarantee your pet will learn, accept, or tolerate a behavior, lifestyle or activity.

An agreement does not guarantee the pet you adopt will be a perfect fit for you.

Problems between you and your bird

"My bird and I come together for the fulfillment of mutual need. If I feel our relationship is not happy, I will adjust our agreement, focusing on the areas which pertain to the problems or challenges we are experiencing."

(Your veterinarian, a certified animal behaviorist, or animal communicator may be able to help you and your bird through a difficult time or situation.)

"In the event happiness cannot be restored, I understand it is my responsibility to find a new guardian and a safe and suitable living arrangement for my bird."

(Surrendering your bird to a shelter, rescue organization, or new owner will end your agreement.)

A Pet Snake

What are your expectations of a pet snake? Snakes are not domesticated animals like dogs or cats. Some snakes are comfortable being held or touched, some are not.

Habitat is critical for all reptiles. You'll need to create the proper environment for your snake to grow and thrive. Check with the breeder, or veterinarian to learn how to create a supportive and nurturing environment for your pet snake.

A snake requires a specific diet, so you'll need to find a reliable food source. Not all veterinarians agree to treat reptiles, so locate a veterinarian *before* you bring your pet snake home.

Exposure to reptiles can put young children and people with a weakened immune system at risk of Salmonellosis infection. Consult with your physician before adopting a reptile.

Your local Herpetological Society is also an excellent source of information about reptiles.

Suggestions for an agreement between you and your snake

Example: *Why I want a pet snake.*

"I've always been fascinated with snakes, I caught snakes in the backyard when I was a kid. A pet snake is perfect for me. I don't like pet hair all over the place, I don't want a pet I have to walk, I don't want to clean a litter box, and I don't like a needy or clingy pet."

"I've decided I want a Ball Python. My friend David has had snakes for over 20 years, he knows where I can get a healthy snake and consistently good food for it. David will also help me create the perfect habitat for my snake."

The agreement should not include behaviors, a lifestyle, or activities which cause the animal physical, mental, or emotional harm.

Visualize your pet snake tolerating admiration and health inspections as you write the agreement.

I want my snake to

You may be able to "condition" your snake to certain behaviors, but you need to be realistic regarding your expectations of a pet snake.

- ▶ Tolerate being admired

- ▶ Tolerate being inspected and kept clean (Some reptiles may never accept being touched).

It may take up to a year or longer for your snake to become comfortable with you and its environment.

I am willing and able to provide the following for my snake

- ▶ Attention

- ▶ A safe and secure home environment

- ▶ A regular routine and feeding schedule

- ▶ A diet which meets my snake's physical needs and requirements

- ▶ The mental stimulation my snake needs

- ▶ Time out of its vivarium, daily if necessary, for good health

- ▶ The environment it needs to be healthy

- An appropriately sized enclosure
- A clean vivarium
- Healthcare, regular physical exams from a veterinarian
- Competent care when I'm away from home for an extended period
- Prearranged care for my snake in the event I'm unable to care for it

Update your agreement

Over the course of your life together, you may need to update the agreement. If there is something in the agreement your snake is unwilling or unable to do, accept or tolerate, remove it from the agreement.

Update the agreement if there's a change in your snake's health. (*Example: Your snake now requires daily medication. Under the section "I am willing and able to give my snake _____." Include how you will care for the snake.*)

Tip: Keep the agreement with your snake's veterinary records. At least once a year—when you take your snake to the veterinarian for an annual exam—review the agreement and update as needed.

An agreement does not guarantee your pet will learn, accept, or tolerate, a behavior, lifestyle or activity.

An agreement does not guarantee the pet you adopt will be a perfect fit for you.

Problems between you and your snake

"My snake and I come together for the fulfillment of mutual need. If I feel our relationship is not happy, I will adjust our agreement focusing on the areas which pertain to the problems or challenges we are experiencing."

(*Your veterinarian, a certified animal behaviorist, or an animal communicator may be able to help you and your snake through a difficult time or situation.*)

"In the event happiness cannot be restored, I understand it is my responsibility to find a new guardian and a safe and suitable living arrangement for my snake."

(Surrendering your snake to a shelter, rescue organization, or new owner will end your agreement.)

A Dog for the Family

Are you planning to adopt a puppy or an adult dog? A puppy will require a significant amount of your time, energy, and patience. Be prepared to make some adjustments in your home environment to accommodate your new puppy or dog.

Dogs like to chew, so cords, wires, small toys, shoes, and plants (among other things). These and other items of this type should be kept out of reach. You can use childproof locks to keep your dog out of cabinets containing food, cleaning products, medications, and garbage.

Do you have a secure yard or outdoor space to walk and exercise a dog? Can you be certain your family dog doesn't run out the door when people are coming in or going out?

Gather as much information about the breed or type of dog you intend to adopt as possible; this is especially important if your family includes a baby or small children. If you have small children, you'll need to show them how to gently handle and interact with the dog. The dog may bite if frightened or if the children play too rough.

Do you already have pets in your household? Consider whether the current pet(s) have ever lived with other animals, specifically dogs?

If a family member has asthma, allergies, or other health conditions consult with their physician before adopting a dog.

You are adopting a dog for the family—however, the agreement will only be between *you* and the dog. Agreements are between the pet and the individual who is ultimately responsible for providing a safe and secure environment, covering the cost of food, supplies, accessories, dog training, and healthcare.

Suggestions for an agreement between you and your family dog

Example: *Why I want a dog for our family.*

"I want my children to have a pet. The dogs I had when I was growing up taught me so much about responsibility, compassion, and love. I want my children to experience the joy of having a dog."

"I've talked to them about adopting a dog from the shelter and they are very excited! I know they will love having a dog to play with and take to the dog park. I'm so excited to watch them grow and learn from having a dog of our own."

The agreement should not include behaviors, a lifestyle, activities or a job which cause the animal physical, mental, or emotional harm.

Visualize the behaviors and activities you would like your dog to learn, accept, and tolerate as you write the agreement.

I want our dog to:

- Participate in obedience training classes
- Learn to respond to commands
- Learn to communicate the need for food and attention
- Learn to communicate fear
- Learn to play fetch and Frisbee
- Learn to walk on-leash
- Learn its name
- Tolerate physical examination from a veterinarian

- Tolerate grooming: bath, haircut, brushing, nails trimmed.

- Tolerate being handled by the children—as long as they do so carefully and gently

- Tolerate sleeping in a crate (Consult a professional dog trainer for information and advice regarding the correct way to crate train your dog.)

It may take up to a year or longer for your dog to become comfortable with you, family members and its environment. Keep this in mind as you list the behaviors, lifestyle, activities or job you would like your dog to learn, accept or tolerate.

I am willing and able to provide the following for our dog

- Attention

- A safe and secure home environment

- A regular routine and feeding schedule, fresh water

- A diet which meets our dog's physical needs and requirements

- The exercise our dog needs daily

- Obedience training classes

- Healthcare, regular physical exams from a veterinarian

- An appropriately sized crate

- Competent care when we are away from home for an extended period: a pet sitter, or boarding kennel.

A job for our dog

The dog you ultimately adopt will be an important factor in this part of the agreement. A puppy will need socialization, obedience training, time to grow, mature, and bond with you and other family members before learning a job. An adult dog will also need training and time to bond with you and other family members before learning a job.

When considering a job for your family dog think about the dog's purpose in your family's life as well as its age, size, breed, natural skills and abilities, temperament, mental and emotional maturity, physical ability, training, and history.

Here's a short list of jobs your family dog could perform

- Be patient and gentle with the children (The children must be gentle with the dog as well.)
- Play with the children
- Alert someone if one of the children needs help
- Pick up its toys
- Carry food bowl
- Avoid jumping up on family members
- Bark when someone knocks or rings the doorbell

Instincts are helpful, but your dog will need training, guidance, and direction to learn a job. *Never correct or discipline your dog with physical punishment or yelling.* If you're having difficulty training your dog, hire a professional dog trainer, they will show you how to work with your dog.

Update your agreement

Over the course of your life together, you will need to update the agreement. If there is something in the agreement your dog is unwilling or unable to do, accept or tolerate, remove it from the agreement.

- Update the agreement when your dog takes on a job *(Describe the job.)*
- Update the agreement if there's a change to your dog's job description
- Update the agreement if your dog stops performing a job
- Update the agreement if there's a change in your dog's health (Example: Your dog now requires daily medication.

Under the section "I am willing and able to give my dog _____." Include - the medication it needs daily.)

Tip: Keep the agreement with your dog's veterinary records. At least once a year—when you take your dog to the veterinarian for an annual exam—review the agreement and update as needed.

An agreement does not guarantee your pet will learn, accept, or tolerate, a behavior, lifestyle, activity or job.

An agreement does not guarantee the pet you adopt will be a perfect fit for you or your family members.

Problems between you or a family member and your dog

"This dog comes to our family for the fulfillment of mutual need. If I feel the relationship between our dog and our family is not a happy one, I will adjust the agreement, focusing on the areas which pertain to the problems or challenges we are experiencing."

(Your veterinarian, a professional dog trainer, certified dog behaviorist, or animal communicator may be able to help you and your dog through a difficult time or situation.)

"In the event happiness cannot be restored, I understand it is my responsibility to find a new guardian and a safe and suitable living arrangement for our dog."

(Surrendering your dog to a shelter, rescue organization, or new owner will end your agreement.)

A Cat for the Family

Are you planning to adopt a kitten or an adult cat? A kitten will require a significant amount of your time, energy, and patience. Be prepared to make some adjustments in your home environment to accommodate your new kitten or cat.

Cords and pulls attached to window coverings should be out of reach and never left hanging. Pick up small items which could be ingested: string, twist ties, puzzle pieces, buttons, jewelry, small toys, etc. Remove poisonous plants. You can use childproof locks to keep your cat out of cabinets containing food, cleaning products, medications, plastic bags, and garbage.

Whether you adopt a cat or kitten, it's a good idea to purchase a scratching post, cat tree, or climbing tower *before* you bring your new cat home. Scratching is an instinctive behavior for cats, they scratch to mark territory, stretch, express emotion, etc. In the *"Questions and Answers"* section, you'll find tips and steps you can take to encourage your cat to use a scratching post or cat tree.

Litter box placement is also an important consideration. I've seen litter boxes in some interesting places: bathtubs, bathroom cupboards, closets, etc. If you put the litter box in a cupboard or closet, you'll need to keep the door open, or cut a hole in the door. A dog can be trained to let you know when it needs to go out, but you likely won't be able to train your cat to let you know when it needs to go outside or use the litter box.

If you have small children, you'll need to show them how to handle the cat gently. The cat may scratch or bite if frightened or if the children play too rough.

If a family member has asthma, allergies, or other health conditions consult with their physician before adopting a cat.

You are adopting a cat for the family, however, the agreement will only be between *you* and the cat. Agreements are between the pet and the individual who is ultimately responsible for providing a safe and secure environment, covering the cost of food, supplies, accessories, and healthcare.

Suggestions for an agreement between you and your family cat

Example: *Why I want for a cat for our family.*

"My daughter Kathy has been asking for a kitten for a few years. I think she's old enough to take on some responsibilities for a pet. A neighbor of ours took in a stray cat and then found out the cat was pregnant. I told Kathy she could have one of the kittens."

"Our neighbor said she'll let us know when the mama cat starts having her babies. I hope Kathy can watch her new kitten being born; it will be a great experience for her to see the birth."

The agreement should not include behaviors, a lifestyle, or activities which cause the animal physical, mental, or emotional harm.

Visualize the behaviors and activities you would like your cat to learn, accept, and tolerate as you write the agreement.

I want our cat to

- ► Let us care for it

- ► Learn to use a scratching post or cat tree. (The cat may still scratch furniture, rugs, and/or carpet.)

- ► Learn to communicate the need for food and attention

- ► Learn to communicate fear

- Learn its name

- Learn interactive play

- Tolerate physical examination from a veterinarian (A visit to the vet can be extremely stressful for some cats. Talk to your veterinarian about how to handle a scared cat.)

- Tolerate being groomed: brushed, nails trimmed (Some cats will not tolerate being groomed.)

- Tolerate being petted by each of the family members

- Tolerate being an indoor cat. (If you desire an indoor cat.)

- Tolerate being admired

- Tolerate being handled by the children, as long as they do so carefully and gently.

It may take up to a year or longer for your cat to become comfortable with you, family members and its environment. Keep this in mind as you list the behaviors, lifestyle, and activities you would like your cat to learn, accept or tolerate.

I am willing and able to provide the following for our cat

- Attention

- A safe and secure home environment

- A regular routine and feeding schedule and fresh water

- A diet which meets our cat's physical needs and requirements

- The play and exercise our cat needs daily (Cats need exercise, especially when they are young.)

- Access to a litter box, which I clean daily

- Healthcare, regular physical exams from a veterinarian

- Competent care when we are away from home for an extended period: a pet sitter, or boarding kennel.

Update your agreement

Over the course of your life together, you may need to update the agreement between you and your family cat. If there is something in the agreement your cat is unwilling or unable to do, accept or tolerate, remove it from the agreement.

Update the agreement if there's a change in your cat's health. (*Example: Your cat now requires daily medication. Under the section "I am willing and able to give my cat _____." Include the name or description of the treatment or medication it needs daily.*)

Tip: Keep the agreement with your cat's veterinary records. At least once a year—when you take your cat to the veterinarian for an annual exam—review the agreement and update as needed.

An agreement does not guarantee your pet will learn, accept, or tolerate a behavior, lifestyle, or activity.

An agreement does not guarantee the pet you adopt will be a perfect fit for you and for your family members.

Problems between you or a family member and your cat

"The cat comes to our family for the fulfillment of mutual need. If I feel the relationship between our cat and our family is not happy, I will adjust the agreement focusing on the areas which pertain to the problems or challenges we are experiencing."

(*Your veterinarian, a certified cat behaviorist, or an animal communicator may be able to help you and your cat through a difficult time or situation.*)

"In the event happiness cannot be restored, I understand it is my responsibility to find a new guardian and a safe and suitable living arrangement for our cat."

(*Surrendering your cat to a shelter, rescue organization, or new owner will end your agreement.*)

A Rabbit for the Family

There are many things you'll need to consider before adopting a rabbit for your family. Be prepared to make some adjustments in your home environment to accommodate your new rabbit.

Rabbits like to chew, so cords, wires, small toys, shoes, and plants, among other things, should be out of reach. You'll also need to rabbit-proof door frames and baseboards.

If you keep your rabbit in a pen or enclosure, you'll need to let it out daily for exercise. Rabbits need a good size area to run, jump, and play. You'll need to brush your rabbit regularly to keep its coat healthy and shiny, and trim its nails a least once a month, depending on how active it is.

Some rabbits may learn to use a litter box, however not all cat litter is safe for rabbits. Check with the breeder, rescue organization, or your veterinarian to learn which type of litter is safe for your rabbit. Having your pet rabbit spayed or neutered may reduce its inclination to spray, chew and dig.

A proper diet is critical for keeping your pet rabbit healthy. Rabbits may live on carrots and lettuce in cartoons, but in real life they need a balanced diet to maintain proper digestion and good health. Check with the breeder, rescue organization, or your veterinarian to learn what to feed your pet rabbit.

If you have small children, you'll need to show them how to handle the rabbit gently, even how to pick it up. A rabbit may scratch or bite if frightened, or if the children play too rough.

If a family member has asthma, allergies, or other health conditions, consult with their physician before adopting a rabbit.

You are adopting a rabbit for the family—however, the agreement will only be between *you* and the rabbit. Agreements are between the pet and the individual who is ultimately responsible for providing a safe and secure environment, covering the cost of food, supplies, accessories, and healthcare.

Suggestions for an agreement between you and your family rabbit

Example: *Why I want two rabbits for our family.*

"I always wanted an Easter Bunny when I was a kid, but my mother didn't want a pet rabbit running around the house. Now *my* kids are asking for a pet rabbit. I've volunteered at an animal shelter for many years, and I've helped care for all types of animals—including rabbits."

"Recently a pair of young rabbits were brought into the shelter. I've never lost my desire to have a rabbit, and now with the kids asking for a rabbit, it feels like the perfect opportunity to get the kids (and myself) a couple of pet rabbits!"

"Having pet rabbits will teach them about responsibility, compassion, and love. I'm excited to see the kids and the rabbits play together."

The agreement should not include behaviors, a lifestyle, or activities which cause the animal physical, mental, or emotional harm.

Visualize the behaviors and activities you would like your rabbits to learn, accept, and tolerate as you write the agreement.

I want our rabbits to

- Let us care for them
- Learn to communicate the need for food and attention
- Learn to communicate fear

- Learn their names
- Tolerate physical examination from a veterinarian
- Tolerate being groomed; brushed, nails trimmed
- Tolerate being admired
- Tolerate being handled by the children—as long as they do so carefully and gently

It may take up to a year or longer for your rabbits to become comfortable with you, family members and their environment. Keep this in mind as you list the behaviors, lifestyle, and activities you would like your rabbits to learn, accept or tolerate.

I am willing and able to provide the following for our rabbits

- Attention…
- A safe and secure home environment
- A regular routine and feeding schedule
- A diet which meets our rabbit's physical needs, and requirements
- An adequately sized hutch
- Time out of their hutch daily for play and exercise
- A clean hutch, daily spot cleaning, and a thorough weekly cleaning
- Healthcare, regular physical exams from a veterinarian
- Competent care when we are away from home for an extended period: a pet sitter, or boarding kennel. (Check availability in your area)

Update your agreement

Over the course of your life together, you may need to update the agreement. Or, if there is something in the original agreement your rabbits prove unwilling or unable to do, accept, or tolerate, remove it from the agreement.

Update the agreement if there's a change in your rabbit's health. (*Example: Your rabbit now requires daily medication. Under the section "I am willing and able to give my rabbit _____." Include the name or description of the treatment or the medication it needs daily.*)

Tip: Keep the agreement with your rabbits' veterinary records. At least once a year—when you take your rabbits to the veterinarian for an annual exam—review the agreement and update as needed.

An agreement does not guarantee your pet will learn, accept or tolerate, a behavior, lifestyle or activity.

An agreement does not guarantee the pet you adopt will be a perfect fit for you.

Problems between you or a family member and your rabbits

"The rabbits come to our family for the fulfillment of mutual need. If I feel the relationship between our rabbits and our family is not happy, I will adjust the agreement, focusing on the areas which pertain to the problems or challenges we are experiencing."

(Your veterinarian, a certified animal behaviorist, or an animal communicator may be able to help you and your rabbits through a difficult time or situation.)

"In the event happiness cannot be restored, I understand it is my responsibility to find a new guardian and a safe and suitable living arrangement for our rabbits."

(Surrendering your rabbits to a shelter, rescue organization, or new owner will end your agreement.)

Guinea Pigs for the Family

There are many things you'll need to consider before adopting a Guinea Pig for your family. Be prepared to make some adjustments in your home environment to accommodate your new Guinea Pigs.

Guinea Pigs like to chew, so electrical cords, wires, small toys, and plants (among other things) should be out of reach. Guinea Pigs need time out of their cage daily for exercise and mental stimulation.

Guinea Pigs' teeth never stop growing—chewing prevents their teeth from getting too long. Check with the breeder, rescue organization or a veterinarian to learn what's safe for your Guinea Pigs to chew on.

Guinea Pigs are temperature sensitive and susceptible to heatstroke, so they should be in a temperature-controlled environment. Guinea Pigs are social animals and do best with a companion Guinea Pig, so consider adopting two Guinea Pigs.

Guinea Pigs groom themselves, but regular brushing will help maintain a healthy coat. Long-haired Guinea Pigs require daily brushing. Your Guinea Pigs will also need their nails clipped.

Your Guinea Pigs will need time and gentle handling to get them used to being touched and picked up. Guinea Pigs have delicate bones, and their legs and body need to be supported when held. Show small children how to gently handle and pick up the Guinea Pigs.

If a family member has asthma, allergies, or other health conditions, consult with their physician before adopting Guinea Pigs. Some people have allergies to the proteins in Guinea Pigs' saliva and urine. Hay and wood shavings in the Guinea Pigs' cage can also cause allergies.

Although you are adopting Guinea Pigs for the family, the agreement will only be between *you* and the Guinea Pigs. Agreements are between the pet(s) and the individual who is ultimately responsible for providing a safe and secure environment, covering the cost of food, supplies, accessories, and healthcare.

Suggestions for an agreement between you and your family Guinea Pigs

Example: *Why I want Guinea Pigs for our family.*

"The kids really want a pet and I want them to have a pet, but our 15th-floor apartment doesn't have any outdoor space, and there's no green space nearby. I don't think it's an ideal situation for a dog, and I'm not comfortable with cats. I think a couple of Guinea Pigs will be a good choice for our family pet."

"I've talked to the kids about getting a couple of Guinea Pigs and they are super excited. I told them they each get to name one of the Guinea Pigs, and we've talked about how they can help care for the Guinea Pigs."

The agreement should not include behaviors, a lifestyle, or activities which cause the animal physical, mental, or emotional harm.

Visualize the behaviors and activities you would like the Guinea Pigs to learn, accept, and tolerate as you write the agreement.

I want our Guinea Pigs to

- ▶ Let us care for them
- ▶ Learn to communicate the need for food and attention
- ▶ Learn to communicate fear
- ▶ Tolerate physical examination from a veterinarian

- Tolerate grooming: brushing, nails trimmed
- Tolerate being admired
- Tolerate being handled by the children—as long as they do so carefully and gently

It may take a few months or longer for your Guinea Pigs to become comfortable with you, family members and their environment. Keep this in mind as your list the behaviors, lifestyle, and activities you would like your Guinea Pigs to learn, accept or tolerate.

I am willing and able to provide the following for our Guinea Pigs

- Attention
- A safe and secure home environment
- A regular routine and feeding schedule
- A diet which meets our Guinea Pigs' physical needs and requirements
- An appropriately sized cage
- Time out of their cage daily for play and exercise, to stretch and explore
- A clean cage, daily spot cleaning, and a thorough weekly cleaning
- Healthcare, regular physical exams from a veterinarian
- Competent care when we are away from home for an extended period: a pet sitter, or boarding kennel. (Check availability in your area).

Update your agreement

Over the course of your life together, you may need to update the agreement. If there is something in the agreement your Guinea Pigs are unwilling or unable to do, accept, or tolerate, remove it from the agreement.

Update the agreement if there's a change in your Guinea Pig's health. (*Example: Your Guinea Pig now requires daily medication. Under the section "I am willing and able to give my Guinea Pig _____." Include the name or description of the treatment or medication it needs daily.*)

Tip: Keep the agreement with your Guinea Pigs' veterinary records. At least once a year—when you take your Guinea Pigs to the veterinarian for an annual exam—review the agreement and update as needed.

An agreement does not guarantee your pets will learn, accept, or tolerate a behavior, lifestyle, or activity.

An agreement does not guarantee the pets you adopt will be a perfect fit for you and your family members.

Problems between you or a family member and your Guinea Pigs.

"The Guinea Pigs come to our family for the fulfillment of mutual need. If I feel the relationship between our Guinea Pigs and our family is not happy, I will adjust the agreement focusing on the areas which pertain to the problems or challenges we are experiencing."

(Your veterinarian, a certified animal behaviorist, or an animal communicator may be able to help you and your Guinea Pigs through a difficult time or situation.)

"In the event happiness cannot be restored, I understand it is my responsibility to find a new guardian and a safe and suitable living arrangement for our Guinea Pigs."

(Surrendering your Guinea Pigs to a shelter, rescue organization, or new owner will end your agreement.)

A Guard Dog for Personal Protection or to Protect Property

There are several breeds which can be trained to be excellent guard dogs. A guard dog needs obedience training plus advanced training. It's imperative you learn how to maintain control of your guard dog.

If you have asthma, allergies, or other health conditions consult with your physician before adopting a dog.

Suggestions for an agreement between you and your guard dog

Example: *Why I want a guard dog.*

"My house sits on a couple of acres, and I have a chicken coop. I love having chickens and selling the eggs. I want a guard dog to let me know if other animals or people get too close to the chicken coop and disturb the chickens."

"I also enjoy hiking in the hills around my property, I will feel much safer if I have a guard dog to accompany me."

The agreement should not include behaviors, a lifestyle, activities or a job which cause the animal physical, mental, or emotional harm.

Visualize the behaviors and activities you would like your dog to learn, accept, and tolerate as you write the agreement.

I want my guard dog to

- Participate in obedience training and advanced dog training
- Learn to respond to commands
- Learn to follow direction
- Learn to communicate the need for food and attention
- Learn to communicate fear or danger
- Learn to walk on-leash
- Learn its name and necessary code words
- Tolerate physical examination from a veterinarian
- Tolerate grooming: bath, haircut, brushing, nails trimmed, teeth brushed, ears cleaned

It may take up to a year or longer for your dog to become comfortable with you, family members and its environment. Keep this in mind as you list the behaviors, lifestyle, activities or job you would like your dog to learn, accept or tolerate.

I am willing and able to provide the following for my dog:

- Attention
- A safe and secure home environment

- A regular routine and feeding schedule, access to fresh water

- A diet which meets my dog's physical needs and requirements

- The exercise it needs daily

- Obedience training and advanced training with a professional dog trainer

- Healthcare, regular physical exams from a veterinarian

- Competent care when I'm away from home for an extended period

- Prearranged care for my dog in the event I'm unable to care for him or her

A job for my guard dog

The breed or type of dog you ultimately adopt will be an important factor in this part of the agreement. A puppy will need socialization, obedience training, time to grow, mature, and bond with you and other family members before learning a job. An adult dog will also need training and time to bond with you and other family members before learning a job. In both cases, the dog will also need advanced training to be a guard dog.

Here's a short list of jobs your guard dog could perform

- Alert me when someone approaches the house or property

- Alert me if a person or animal approaches a specific area on my property

Instincts are helpful, but your dog will need training, guidance, and direction to learn a job. *Never correct or discipline your dog with physical punishment or yelling.* If you're having difficulty training your dog, hire a professional dog trainer, they will show you how to work with your dog.

Update your agreement

Over the course of your life together, you will need to update the agreement. If there is something in the agreement your dog is unwilling or unable to do, accept or tolerate, remove it from the agreement.

- ▶ Update the agreement when your dog takes on a job (Describe the job.)

- ▶ Update the agreement if there's a change to your dog's job description

- ▶ Update the agreement if your dog stops performing a job

- ▶ Update the agreement if there's a change in your dog's health (Example: Your dog now requires daily medication. Under the section "I am willing and able to give my dog_____." Include the name or description of any treatment or the medication he or she needs daily.)

Tip: Keep the agreement with your dog's veterinary records. At least once a year—when you take your dog to the veterinarian for an annual exam—review the agreement and update as needed.

An agreement does not guarantee your pet will learn, accept, or tolerate, a behavior, lifestyle, activity or job.

An agreement does not guarantee the pet you adopt will be a perfect fit for you.

Problems between you and your guard dog

"My dog and I come together for the fulfillment of mutual need. If I feel our relationship is not happy, I will adjust our agreement, focusing on the areas which pertain to the problems or challenges we are experiencing."

(Your veterinarian, a professional dog trainer, certified dog behaviorist, or animal communicator may be able to help you and your dog through a difficult time or situation.)

"In the event happiness cannot be restored, I understand it is my responsibility to find a new guardian and a safe and suitable living arrangement for my dog."

(Surrendering your dog to a shelter, rescue organization, or new owner will end your agreement.)

A Dog for Show and Breeding

Suggestions for an agreement between you and your show dog

Example: *Why I want a show dog.*

"I love dogs and dog shows! Some of my favorite memories from childhood are of going to dog shows with Uncle Larry and watching his champion poodles compete. I understand the world of showing and breeding dogs, and I'm lucky to have met some of the best handlers."

"I now have a young purebred Australian Shepherd of my own. He looks to be show quality and I'm excited to have the experience of showing my own dog."

The agreement should not include behaviors, a lifestyle, activities or a job which cause the animal physical, mental, or emotional harm.

Handlers do not need an agreement with your show dog. The agreement is only between you and your dog. Agreements are between the pet and the individual who is ultimately responsible for providing a safe and secure environment, covering the cost of food, supplies, accessories, dog training, and healthcare.

Visualize the behaviors and activities you would like your dog to learn, accept, and tolerate as you write the agreement.

I want my show dog to

- Participate in obedience training
- Participate in show dog training
- Respond to learned commands
- Follow the direction of myself and handlers
- Develop a respectful attitude toward me
- Develop a respectful attitude toward handlers and judges
- Participate in regular exercise
- Learn to communicate the need for food and attention
- Learn to communicate fear
- Tolerate physical examination from a veterinarian or a judge.
- Tolerate being groomed: bathing, trimming/styling, brushing, nails trimmed, etc.
- Tolerate traveling and spending time in a crate.
- Tolerate sleeping in a crate. (Consult a professional dog trainer for information and advice regarding the correct way to crate train your dog.)
- Tolerate large crowds
- Tolerate lots of noise
- Tolerate being handled and examined by people

It may take up to a year or longer for your dog to become comfortable with you, family members and its environment. Keep this in mind as you list the behaviors, lifestyle, activities or job you would like your dog to learn, accept or tolerate.

I am willing and able to provide the following for my show dog

- Attention
- A safe and secure home environment
- A regular routine and feeding schedule
- A diet which meets my dog's physical needs and requirements
- The exercise it needs daily
- All necessary training classes with professional trainers
- Professional handlers who respect him, handle him with dignity, protect him, and provide a clean and safe environment when traveling
- Time off to play, rest, and just be a dog
- An appropriately sized crate for sleeping and travel
- Healthcare, regular physical exams from a veterinarian
- Female dog: protection during her estrus cycle to avoid unwanted pregnancies
- Competent care if I'm away from home for an extended period
- Retirement when appropriate for my dog, or if my dog's behavior tells me he no longer wants to show
- Prearranged care for my dog in the event I'm unable to care for him.

Breeding – I am willing and able to provide the following for my dog

- Before breeding, I will have my dog tested for inheritable disease/conditions and health problems
- I will not require my dog to endure any unnatural procreation process which may cause harm or pain.

► I will refrain from breeding practices which may cause harm or compromise my dog's health, or the health of future offspring.

► I will provide Veterinary care during pregnancy and delivery if necessary.

► I will provide care and assistance as needed during the whelping process.

► I will provide competent supervision and veterinarian care for puppies.

► I will provide my female dog retirement from breeding when age appropriate; or if she shows signs of difficulty with pregnancy or giving birth.

► My male dog will be retired from breeding when appropriate for him.

Here's a short list of jobs for a show dog

A puppy will need socialization, obedience training, time to grow, mature, and bond with you before learning jobs.

► Follow the directions and commands of trainers and handlers

► Perform at dog shows

► Travel to dog shows

Update your agreement

Over the course of your life together, you will need to update the agreement. If there is something in the agreement your dog is unwilling or unable to do, accept, or tolerate, remove it from the agreement.

► Update the agreement when your dog takes on a job (Describe the job.)

► Update the agreement if there's a change to your dog's job description

► Update the agreement if your dog stops performing a job

► Update the agreement when your dog retires

► Update the agreement if there's a change in your dog's health. (Example: Your dog now requires daily medication. Under the section "I am willing and able to give my dog _____." Include the name of a medication or a description of the treatment he needs daily.)

Tip: Keep the agreement with your dog's veterinary records. At least once a year, when you take your dog to the veterinarian for an annual exam, review the agreement and update as needed.

An agreement does not guarantee your pet will learn, accept, or tolerate, a behavior, lifestyle, activity or job.

An agreement does not guarantee the pet you adopt will be a perfect fit for you.

Problems between you and your show dog.

"My dog and I come together for the fulfillment of mutual need. If I feel our relationship is not happy, I will adjust our agreement, focusing on the areas which pertain to the problems or challenges we are experiencing."

(Your veterinarian, a professional dog trainer, certified dog behaviorist, or animal communicator may be able to help you and your dog through a difficult time or situation.)

"In the event happiness cannot be restored, I understand it is my responsibility to find a new guardian and a safe and suitable living arrangement for my dog."

(Surrendering your dog to a shelter, rescue organization, or new owner will end your agreement.)

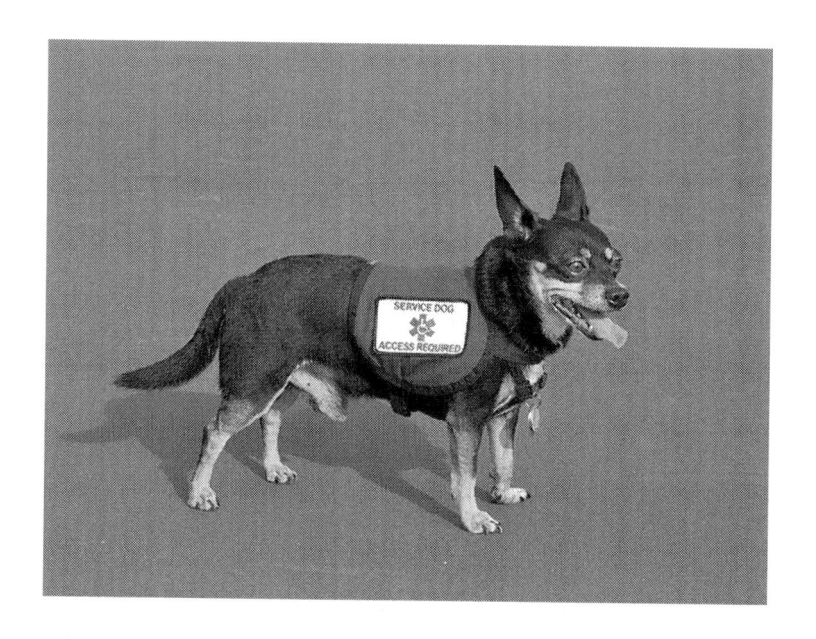

Service Dogs

The following is a partial list of common types of service dogs and *some* of the services they are trained to do for their handler.

Guide dogs for visual disabilities are trained to

- ▶ Follow voice and hand signals

- ▶ Assist handler when boarding public transportation

- ▶ Assist handler when walking: navigate and steer around obstacles

- ▶ Assist handler when climbing stairs

- ▶ Assist handler outside the home: navigate public spaces, going to work, etc.

Hearing/Signal dogs are trained to

- ▶ Alert handler when the phone rings

- ▶ Alert handler to a knock on the door, or the sound of a doorbell

- Alert handler of smoke or security alarm

Autism service dogs are trained to:

- Stop a child from wandering or running away
- Interrupt self-harming behaviors
- Respond to repetitive behaviors
- Alert handler to a knock on the door, or the sound of a doorbell
- Alert handler of smoke or security alarm
- Apply physical pressure to calm anxiety: step on handler's foot, put paws on the handler's lap, lay on the handler

Mobility assist dogs are trained to

- Provide a counterbalance for stability, help handler get out of a chair, to stand or sit down
- Retrieve and deliver dropped items: keys, remote control, shoes, etc.
- Assist handler using a walker
- Open doors: push buttons for the handler
- Turn lights on and off for handler
- Pull a lightweight manual wheelchair
- Carry a backpack

Seizure Response and Medical Alert dogs are trained to

- Provide Seizure alert, sense handler's impending seizure
- Glucose alert, sense handler's change in glucose levels
- Summon help when handler has a seizure or medical problem
- Carry information about handler's medical condition

- ▶ Service dogs for veterans are trained to
- ▶ Assist with various symptoms of PTSD
- ▶ Provide stability, help handler out of a chair, when standing or sitting down
- ▶ Apply physical pressure to calm anxiety
- ▶ Stand between handler and another person
- ▶ Enter unfamiliar area or space before the handler
- ▶ Retrieve and deliver dropped items: keys, remote control, shoes, etc.
- ▶ Open doors: push buttons for the handler
- ▶ Turn lights on and off for handler
- ▶ Carry a backpack
- ▶ Pull a lightweight manual wheelchair

* Therapy dogs are not service dogs *

Therapy dogs offer comfort to people in hospitals, nursing homes, senior centers, physical rehabilitation facilities, group homes, hospice, certain public spaces such as schools, libraries, courts and disaster areas. Here's a list of a few temperament guidelines and skills for a therapy dog

- ▶ People-oriented
- ▶ Easily adjust to walking on unfamiliar surfaces
- ▶ Calm around wheelchairs, people walking with canes and walkers
- ▶ Undisturbed by strange sounds, and loud noise
- ▶ Relaxed in new and unfamiliar environments
- ▶ Comfortable being handled and touched
- ▶ Sociable and patient with people
- ▶ Calm around children
- ▶ Comfortable around other dogs

A Guide Dog

Enhanced mobility, independence, confidence, companionship, and a greater sense of security are some of the many benefits you'll experience with your Guide dog.

You will have a contract with the organization from which you acquired your dog. You may want to create an agreement between you and your guide dog as well.

Suggestions for an agreement between you and your guide dog

Example: *Why I want a guide dog.*

"I began losing my vision about 10 years ago, I have a hard time getting around and going to public places. I'm a very social person, but my vision problem has made it difficult to go places and do the things I used to do."

"I'm so excited about my guide dog! Having a guide dog will bring back some of the independence I used to have—and the companionship will be great!"

The agreement should not include behaviors, a lifestyle, activities or a job which cause the animal physical, mental, or emotional harm. *(Your guide dog will go through guide dog training classes before coming to you. You and your dog will also train together.)*

I want my guide dog to

- Learn to work with me when we train together
- Learn to communicate the need for food and attention
- Learn to communicate fear or caution
- Tolerate physical examination from a veterinarian
- Tolerate being groomed; bath, trim, brushing, nails trimmed, etc.
- Tolerate being a guide dog

I am willing and able to provide the following for my dog

In this section, you may want to include the instructions and responsibilities determined by the organization from which you acquired your dog.

- A safe and secure home environment
- A regular routine and feeding schedule and fresh water
- A diet which meets my dog's physical needs and requirements
- Proper handling, utilizing the skills and handling techniques I learn in training classes
- Post training classes for both of us; and/or a refresher course at the training facility if necessary
- Good care: Fulfill my responsibilities for my guide dog as per the contract I have with the organization from which I acquire my dog
- Healthcare, a regular physical exam from a veterinarian, as per the contract I have with the organization from which I acquire my dog

- Competent care in the event we are separated for a short time, as per the contract I have with the organization from which I acquire my guide dog

- Retirement when appropriate for my dog as per the contract I have with the organization from which I acquired my guide dog

My guide dog's jobs include the following

Your dog will be trained for many jobs as well as how to respond in a variety of situations. You may want to list some of the specific jobs your dog performs for you.

Example:

- Assist me when boarding public transportation
- Assist me when navigating streets
- Assist me with stairs
- Go with me to the grocery store, coffee shop, work, etc.
- Paw at me when it needs to go outside
- Bark when someone knocks or rings the doorbell
- Pick up small objects I drop
- Bring the phone to me

Update your agreement

Over the course of your life together, you will need to update your personal agreement with your service dog. If there is something in the personal agreement between you and your dog which your dog is unwilling or unable to do, accept or tolerate, remove it from the agreement.

- Update the agreement when your dog takes on a new job (Describe the job.)
- Update the agreement if there's a change to your dog's job description
- Update the agreement if your dog stops performing a job

▶ Update the agreement when your dog retires (If you decide to keep the dog.)

Tip: Keep the agreement with your dog's veterinary records. At least once a year—when you take your dog to the veterinarian for an annual exam, review the agreement and update as needed.

An agreement does not guarantee your pet will learn, accept, or tolerate, a behavior, lifestyle, activity or job.

Problems between you and your guide dog

This needs to be handled according to the contract you have with the organization that provided your dog.

More Information about Pets in this Book

Dogs—If you're considering adopting a dog, you need to think about your lifestyle. Consider your home environment, work schedule, the amount of physical activity you're comfortable with, and the time and energy you'll have to devote to your new best friend. The *average* lifespan of a dog is about 10-12 years, but of course, how long a dog lives depends on its health and lifestyle.

Obedience Training—Obedience training provides mental stimulation and physical activity for your dog. Your dog will learn basic commands such as: sit, stay, come, down, leave it, and you will learn how to effectively communicate with your dog. Good communication between you and your dog is the foundation of a happy and healthy relationship.

Socialization—Think about how you want the dog you adopt to interact with your world. Do you share your home with other adults, children, or pets? Is your home environment very active with lots of people coming and going? Do you have a busy social life? Would you like your dog to accompany you to work, when visiting friends, on vacations, to restaurants, parks, and outdoor events?

The optimum socialization period for dogs ranges from about 3 to 12 weeks of age. If you're adopting a puppy, you'll likely bring your new puppy home when it's about eight weeks old. This is a good time to begin to introduce your puppy to new people, animals, sounds, situations, and activities you enjoy.

Ask the breeder, rescue organization, shelter staff, or the person from whom you acquire the puppy about the environment the puppy lived in during the first eight weeks of its life. If possible, find out if the puppy has been with its littermates and if it's been exposed to children and other animals. Ask if it has spent time indoors and outdoors.

Liability—It is estimated one-third of all homeowner insurance liability claims are for dog bites. Not all insurance companies cover all dog breeds, so check with your insurance company about including your dog under the liability portion of your homeowner's or renter's insurance policy. Obedience training and socialization are proactive steps you can take to help avoid a claim on your insurance.

Cats—If you're considering adopting a cat, you'll need to decide if you want your cat to be an indoor cat, outdoor cat, or both? Unless your cat will be an outdoor cat only, it's a good idea to have a litter box in the house. Keeping the litter box clean will encourage your cat to use it. If the litter box is not cleaned often, your cat may look for other places in your house to do its business.

I've had cats for many years and I've moved a lot. When I preview a potential new home, I automatically look for a place to put the litter box. If the house or apartment doesn't accommodate my pet's needs as well as my own, it's not the right place for us. Food and water bowls should be kept in a separate location, away from the litter box.

Consider your furniture *before* adopting a cat. Scratching is an instinctive behavior for cats and there are no guarantees your cat won't scratch the furniture, drapes or carpet, even if it has a scratching post or cat tree.

The estrus cycle (when the cat is in heat) is another important factor to think about. The first estrus cycle usually occurs between 6 to 12 months of age, and then twice a year often in the spring and fall. The cycle lasts from 3 to 14 days, but if the cat is not mated, she may go into heat again within several days. It can be extremely challenging to keep a cat indoors (to avoid pregnancy) when she's in heat. You will also have to deal with loud mewing and vocalizing, especially at night. It's best for everyone concerned to have your cat spayed if you're not planning to breed her.

If you adopt a cat, it is important you understand some cats bond more with their environment than with those with whom they share a home.

The average lifespan of an *indoor* cat is about 15 years, but of course, how long a cat lives depends on its health and lifestyle.

Rabbits—Think twice before you run out and adopt a pet rabbit for a child. Rabbits are not necessarily fond of being handled and can bite and scratch when frightened, stressed or mishandled.

Proper handling is very important as a rabbit's spine can easily be damaged if picked up incorrectly. Domestic rabbits are sensitive to temperature, especially heat, so consider keeping your pet rabbit indoors.

There are more than 60 breeds of rabbits. The average size of an adult rabbit is about 6 lbs. The life span of a rabbit is around seven to ten years but, of course, how long a rabbit lives will depend on its health and lifestyle.

Birds—If you're considering adopting a bird, you'll have a wide range of species to choose from. Size and lifespan can vary widely, so do some research before you settle on the bird you want.

Cockatoos are typically a medium to large size bird ranging from 12 to 21 inches in length. They have an average lifespan of 50 to 70 years. Are you prepared to make such a lengthy commitment? I knew a man who adopted a Cockatoo because he wanted a pet that would outlive him, so he'd never have to go through the pain of losing his pet. Hopefully he arranged for his bird to be re-homed and cared for in the event he passed before his bird!

The average size of a Parakeet is about 6 to 7 inches, the lifespan is 12 to 15 years. The lifespan of a bird will depend on its health and lifestyle.

Reptiles—If you consider adopting a reptile it is imperative you first research and educate yourself about the type of reptile you want, and the specific care, food and habitat it requires to live a healthy life.

Some species of reptiles grow to be quite large and may require a significant amount of square footage to get the daily exercise they need to be healthy. Before you decide to adopt a young reptile of any species, you should know the size of the adult version, and how fast it will grow. If you're adopting more than one reptile, make sure you purchase a cage or tank large enough to accommodate multiple reptiles.

The purchase price of some reptiles can be quite low but acquiring everything you need to create the proper habitat for your new reptile can be surprisingly pricey. Environmental requirements may include temperature control, adequate humidity, proper ventilation, an external heat source, proper light exposure, and more. If you adopt a reptile that likes to climb, consider providing artificial vines and branches.

Some cities and states restrict owning or breeding certain species of reptile; check for restrictions in your area *before* you acquire/adopt a pet reptile. The average lifespan varies greatly from species to species, so it's important you know the expected life span of a reptile you plan to adopt. The lifespan of a reptile will depend on its health and lifestyle.

When something is not right in your pet's world.

Sudden destructive behavior, a relapse into bad behavior, separation anxiety, house-training regression, refusal to use the litter box, excessive barking or meowing, may be your pet's way of letting you know something is not right in its world. A change in behavior related to eating, sleeping, or house-training could also signal your pet is having a health problem.

It's almost a knee-jerk reaction for people to blame their pet for "bad" behavior and be completely unaware of how their own behavior or lifestyle could be causing problems for their pet. Before attempting to correct the unwanted behavior, stop and think about what is happening in your world.

Think about any recent changes to your routine related to a demanding work schedule, outside commitments, family obligations, a health issue, or frequent travel. Have there been changes within your household? A family member moving out or an addition to the family—a new partner, baby, or pet moving in? Change can be confusing and unsettling for a pet and trigger stress, fear, anxiety, and depression.

If regular time spent with your pet is suddenly interrupted, your pet may experience separation anxiety, feel bored, insecure, or neglected. Insufficient exercise can also be at the root of many behavior problems; consider whether your pet is getting enough exercise and mental stimulation.

For some pets, (especially cats) moving can be quite traumatic. Animals feel vulnerable and uncertain with the unfamiliar sounds and smells of a new environment. Your pet will need time to adjust to its new surroundings, and lots of attention and reassurance from his or her family.

Example: A person moves into a new home with their indoor cat. A couple of months go by and they notice the cat is sleeping more than usual. She doesn't want to play, hers appetite has decreased a little, and she's not interested in looking out of the windows. They remember how much their cat enjoyed looking out of the second story windows in the condo they lived in previously. The cat loved to sit on the windowsill and watch the birds flying around outside and the people walking down below.

The person becomes increasingly anxious about the cat's behavior and wonders if the cat is experiencing a health problem? They take the cat to the veterinarian, but the vet finds nothing wrong with the cat and merely suggests trying different food to entice the cat to eat. They follow the vet's suggestion and try different food, but the cat isn't excited about the new food. She's still sleeping more than usual, and she remains uninterested in play or looking outside.

Their new home is a single-story house with a yard. The person expected the cat would be eager to watch the birds picking at the seeds on the ground, the squirrels scurrying up and down the trees, and lizards sunning themselves on the patio. The person wonders if the cat is stressed and a little frightened because now everything outside is up close and at the same level.

The person decides to try giving their cat more time and attention each day, hoping to reassure the cat that she is safe and secure in their new home. Soon the cat is back to its old self, her appetite has increased, she's playing again, and watching the birds, squirrels, and lizards outside.

If you are unable to keep your pet; preparing for the unexpected.

Whether you adopt a pet from a shelter, rescue organization, breeder, friend or pet store find out if you can return the animal if necessary. Usually people adopt a pet with the intention of providing a forever home for the animal, but sometimes things just don't work out.

Example: A sudden job or career change necessitates the need for a long-distance move and you're unable to take the pet with you. You lose your job and can no longer afford to have a pet. Your pet develops a chronic health problem and you can't afford ongoing treatment and medication. You or a family member develops allergies to the pet. A family member becomes ill and you need to relocate or be away for an extended time.

Or, more examples: You find yourself unexpectedly pregnant and don't feel you'll be able to handle a new baby and a pet. Or, you feel uncomfortable about the pet being around a new baby. The pet is aggressive toward your children or your children don't like the pet. The new pet you'd like to add to your household is aggressive toward other pets. Or, the pet you had before you adopted the new pet will not accept sharing space with the new pet, and is acting aggressively toward it.

You find caring for the pet demands much more of your time and energy than you expected, or you're not able to adjust your lifestyle enough to accommodate your pet's needs.

Returning a pet is difficult for all concerned—especially the pet—but it's not okay to keep an animal in a difficult, oppressive, deprived or abusive situation either. No one likes to feel unwanted, it's not right to force a pet to stay in a situation where it is not properly cared for and loved.

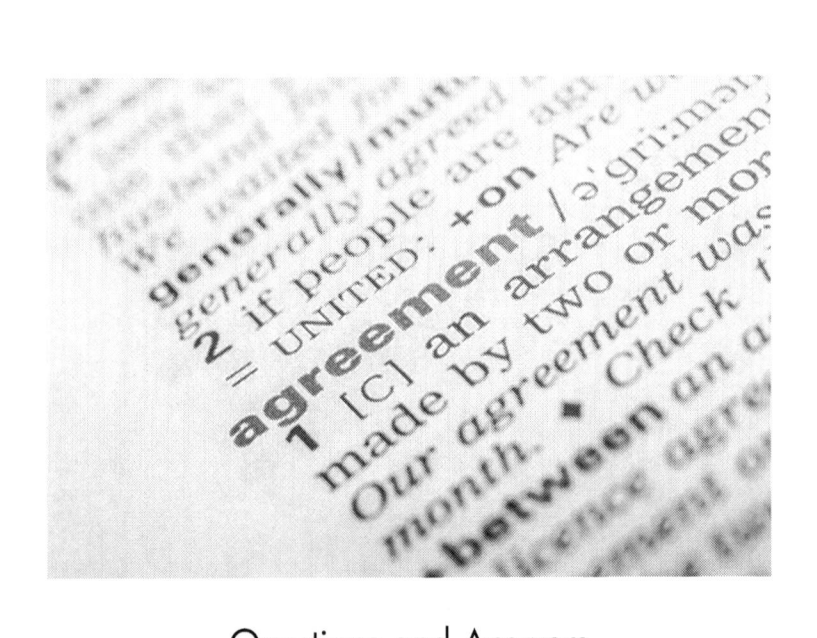

Questions and Answers

Is it okay to adopt just one parakeet?

Wild parakeets live in flocks and are naturally social birds. As pets, parakeets often to do better paired with another parakeet. A pair of parakeets will have each other for companionship and play, but they still need at least an hour a day of interaction with their human family. Also factor in time each day for cage cleaning and feeding. A good diet for your parakeet includes fresh fruits and vegetables. Birdseed alone is not a healthy diet for your parakeet.

You'll find lots of bird paraphernalia to help you to create a fun, interesting, and stimulating environment inside your parakeet's cage: perches, ladders, swings, hoops, bells, etc. Check with the breeder, rescue organization or veterinarian to make sure the items you're planning to put in your bird's cage are safe and non-toxic to your parakeet.

A good environment inside your parakeet's cage is great, but it may also enjoy time out of its cage. Be sure to take precautions to ensure your bird's safety before letting it out of its cage. Close doors and windows, extinguish candles, remove any plants or flowers which could be harmful if ingested. Move to another room other pets which could be threatening or dangerous to your parakeet.

What's the difference between a Guinea Pig and a Hamster?

They are both rodents, but they are an entirely different species. Guinea Pigs are native to South America. Hamsters are native to Southeast Europe, Asia, and the Middle East. Golden hamsters come from Syria. Here are a few of the differences to consider before adopting a Guinea Pig or hamster.

Guinea Pigs are larger than hamsters. An adult Guinea Pig weighs between two and a half to three pounds, an adult hamster weighs between five and seven ounces. The average lifespan of a Guinea Pig is five to seven years. The average lifespan for a hamster is two to three years.

How old should a child be to have a pet Guinea Pig?

The answer depends on the maturity level of your child, but in general, children should be at least seven years old. A child can *help* with the care and feeding of the Guinea Pigs, but ultimately an adult must be responsible for the care and well-being of the Guinea Pigs. Guinea Pigs tend to be active during the day, but they still may disturb a sleeping child if sharing the same room.

If you adopt a Guinea Pig for a seven-year-old child, the Guinea Pig may live until the child is twelve or fourteen. Think about all the changes your child will go through during those years. A pet that is exciting and interesting to a seven-year-old may not be so captivating for a twelve- or fourteen-year-old.

Guinea Pigs can become lonely and bored without a companion Guinea Pig, so consider adopting two Guinea Pigs. Two Guinea Pigs will have each other for companionship and play but they will still need daily interaction with their human family. Two females, or a male and female, will likely get along better than two males. If you adopt a male and a female, you'll need to have them spayed and neutered unless you want *lots* of baby Guinea pigs.

Do rabbits really purr?

Yes, rabbits purr! Most people think rabbits are quiet, but rabbits communicate with a variety of sounds. They purr or softly and grind their teeth when they're happy and content. Male rabbits purr when they want to breed. Rabbits growl, squeal, scream or hiss when they are angry or frightened. "Thumping," that is, pounding one leg against the floor, may indicate your rabbit is feeling aggressive, anxious or threatened and may bite.

Can I train my cat to do a job?

Probably not. Of course, there are always exceptions, but it would be the exception and not the rule. People have kept cats to keep rodent populations under control throughout history, but it's instinct that makes a cat a good mouser, not training. Adopting a cat with the intention of training it to do a job would be a difficult proposition and could create some real challenges to your relationship with your cat. Only the agreements which pertain to dogs include a job.

Does my child need an agreement with a pet?

A child does *not* need an agreement with a pet, but the child should be a part of the family conversation about a pet. Allow your child to contribute one wish (appropriate for the animal) to the agreement. Agreements are between the pet and the individual who is ultimately responsible for providing a safe and secure environment, covering the cost of food, supplies, accessories, and healthcare.

It is the job of the parents or caregivers to require the child not harm or torment a pet, and to make sure the animal does not bite or hurt the child or any other person.

If the child is in "4-H" activities, and responsible for an animal, then the child may have an agreement with the animal.

How can I stop my cat from scratching on the furniture?

Scratching is an instinctive behavior for cats, they scratch to mark territory, stretch, show emotion, etc. This is not a behavior you can or should try to stop your cat from doing, however, there are steps you can take to persuade your cat to use a scratching post or cat tree. The steps are the same for a kitten or a newly adopted adult cat.

Your cat should have a scratching post, kitty condo, climbing tower or cat tree. There are lots of varieties and sizes on the market, most are covered with carpet, some also have corrugated cardboard, and/or sisal rope. The various materials are to encourage your cat to scratch on the scratching post, kitty condo, climbing tower or cat tree instead of your furniture.

Scratching posts, kitty condos, climbing towers, and cat trees serve multiple purposes which may help coax or persuade your cat to use them. The top level of a cat tree or climbing tower makes a nice perch for your cat to sit and observe everything happening below, and it's also a good place for a nap.

If you have two cats, cat trees, climbing towers, and condos can be a fun play area. For indoor cats a cat tree or climbing tower placed close to a secure window makes a nice lookout spot for your cat to watch the birds, other animals, and people moving around outside.

Kittens especially love to climb, so be aware if you place a cat tree or climbing tower too close to a window with drapes, curtains or blinds. Your kitten or cat may consider it a great launching pad to climb the drapes to get even higher!

If your cat develops neurological problems which cause it to have difficulty balancing, or if it's too old to attempt to navigate climbing up and down a cat tree or tower, you'll need to replace it with a short kitty condo or scratching post.

Once you have the scratching post, kitty condo, climbing tower, or cat tree in place, you need to teach your cat when to use it. Every time the cat scratches on the furniture (or wherever you don't want the cat to scratch), firmly say, "NO," and then move the cat to the appropriate scratching material. As you move the cat, create an image in your mind of the cat scratching on its scratching post, condo, tower, or tree. *Never correct or discipline your cat with physical punishment or yelling.*

During the first few weeks after you bring your new cat home, put the cat on the scratching post, condo, tower, or tree multiple times during the day. You don't have to wait for the cat to sink its claws into the sofa. Rubbing catnip on the scratching surfaces and poles may encourage your cat to use its new scratching post, etc.

Be sure to praise your cat and use treats (if your cat responds to them) when it uses the post, condo, tower, or tree. Positive reinforcement can go a long way in training your cat to learn a new behavior.

Changing the behavior of a pet can be challenging and requires your patience and persistence. In this case, hopefully the scratching post, kitty condo, climbing tower or cat tree will be enticing enough to lure your cat away from scratching on the furniture. There are also sprays, tape and covers you can put on furniture to stop your cat from scratching—this may or may not work. Scratching is an instinctive behavior and it can be difficult to override nature.

It may take up to a year or longer for a new pet to become comfortable with you, family members and its environment. Keep this in mind when you attempt to train your cat to learn a new behavior.

What should I do if the agreement with my dog is not working?

The agreement should not include behaviors, a lifestyle, activities, or a job which cause the animal physical, mental, or emotional harm.

Carefully review the, *"I am willing and able to provide the following for my dog:"* section of the agreement to make sure you are fulfilling your part of the agreement. If your pet is behaving in ways you find inappropriate or difficult, ask yourself if your pet is getting enough attention, exercise, and mental stimulation?

Routine is important for pets. They need regular meals and sleep, consistent play and exercise, and quality time with their person/people to feel safe and secure. If your schedule is erratic, you may need to figure out how you can create a regular routine for your pet. You can't expect your pet will always be able to accommodate your routine or schedule.

If the problem falls under the *"I want my dog to:"* section of the agreement, think about how long you have had your dog. If it's been less than one year since you adopted your dog or wrote the agreement, your dog may need more time to become comfortable with you and its environment. Has your dog had obedience training? Does it respond to commands? It may need more training to learn new behaviors.

If you've attempted to train your dog and it seems unable to unwilling to follow your direction, the problem may be related to your training technique. *Never correct or discipline your dog with physical punishment or yelling.* Hire a professional dog trainer to show you how to work with your dog.

Example: Your dog won't tolerate you trimming its nails. First, make sure you're not trimming the nails too short, this will cause pain and bleeding. Or, if you've had the dog less than one year, it may still be acclimating to its new environment, and not yet feel secure, safe and bonded with you.

You may need to let a professional dog groomer trim your dog's nails for a while. Give your dog a few months with the groomer and then try again. Lots of treats and positive reinforcement during the grooming process may help coax your dog into allowing you to trim its nails or perform other grooming tasks.

If the problem falls under the, *"A job for my dog:"* section of the agreement, consider how long have you had your dog. If it's been less than one year since you adopted your dog or wrote the agreement, your dog may need more time to become comfortable with you and its environment.

Ask yourself the following questions, "Is my dog physically mature enough to do a job?" "Is my dog emotionally mature enough to take on a job?" "Does my dog understand and follow basic obedience commands?" "Could my dog have a health problem that would inhibit or prevent it from performing a job?"

If you have attempted to train your dog to learn a job and the training has not progressed as you had hoped or expected, it is probably time to hire a professional dog trainer to show you how to work with your dog.

An agreement does not guarantee your pet will learn, accept, or tolerate a behavior, lifestyle, activity, or job.

Your veterinarian, a professional dog trainer, certified dog behaviorist, or animal communicator may be able to help you and your dog through a difficult time or situation

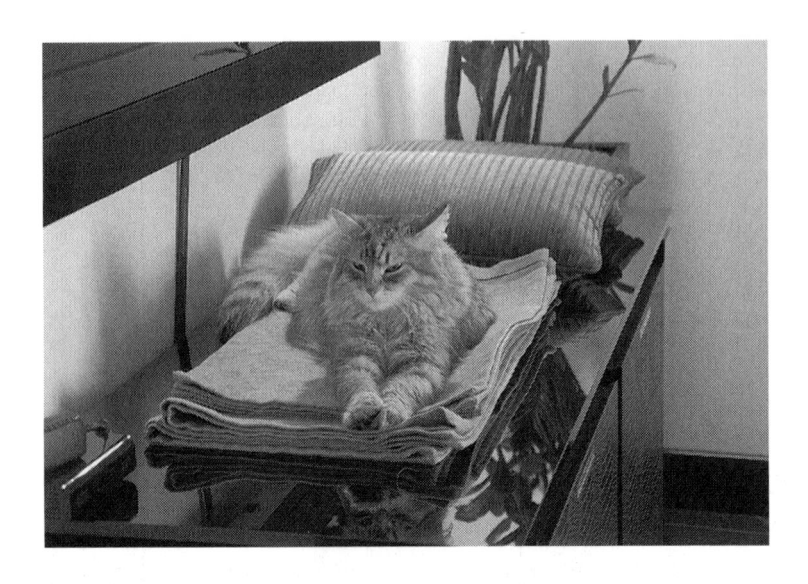

A Staycation for Your Pet

A staycation can be a good alternative to boarding your pet. If you have a pet sitter, trusted neighbor or friend who can act as guardian and caregiver to your pet while you're away. You should feel comfortable with this person entering your home alone, and you should feel confident they will take good care of your pet.

It's best if the caregiver can meet with you and your pet in your home at least once before you travel. Walk them through the process of caring for your pet and show them where all pet related supplies are kept. Leave all instructions and information in your home for the caregiver, in case they forget something.

The person caring for your pet will need feeding instructions: feeding times, where your pet normally eats, portion size, location of food, bowls, and utensils if needed. Show them where the leash and poop bags are kept if you want them to walk your dog. If you have a cat, show them where the litter box is located as well as related essentials; scoop, waste can, extra litter and cleaning supplies for accidents.

Provide veterinarian information and show them the location of your pet's travel carrier. If your pet requires medication, the caregiver should have experience administering the type of medication your pet needs. You must know before you leave if your pet will accept medicine from the caregiver.

Give them the name and address of a local boarding kennel, in the event your pet needed to be evacuated from your home and transferred to a boarding facility. Kennels often require animals to be up to date with vaccinations before admittance, the caregiver will need a copy of current vaccination records. Make sure your pet's microchip information is current.

The caregiver will need your cell phone number and/or another number where you can be reached day or night. It's also a good idea to give them the name and number of a local friend or relative they can call if they need assistance with your pet.

People and animals are brought together for a purpose.

I believe animals connect with specific people, just as people connect with certain individuals. Each has something the other needs to learn, or there's an experience that needs to be shared. When we find a stray animal or an animal finds us, I believe it's because we are supposed to connect with each other. Our connection may only last long enough to take the animal to a safe and secure shelter, but there's always a reason.

Many of us have been adopted by a stray animal and often this connection occurs during a pivotal point in our life. A few years ago, I was "adopted" by a darling long-haired, orange and white cat; she subsequently became one of the greatest joys of my life. I already had an indoor cat the day this cat arrived on my front porch, and I was not thinking about getting another cat at the time. My current cat was not friendly toward other cats and I didn't know if she would accept living with another cat.

It was a beautiful summer evening, my cat liked to sit by the front screen door and look outside. I was on the phone with a friend when I heard loud meowing and hissing coming from the living room. I walked into the living room and over to the front door and sitting on the porch was a darling long-haired orange and white cat. My cat was *not* impressed (at least not in a good way) with this feline interloper. She wanted nothing to do with it and she wanted it off her property!

I lived in a neighborhood where nearly everyone had a pet, so I assumed the cat belonged to one of my neighbors. I told the cat to go home and closed the front door. I waited a little while, looked out the living room window and the cat was still sitting on the porch. I checked again before I went to bed and it was still there.

The next morning, I looked out the window, but I didn't see the cat anywhere. Relieved and a little disappointed I assumed it had gone home, but as soon as I opened the front door, the cat ran down the trunk of a tree in the front yard and right up to the screen door. In the light of day, I could see it was young, I was glad it had spent the night in the tree, safe from any wandering neighborhood dogs or other cats.

It was just the cutest little cat, I wanted to scoop it up in my arms and bring it into the house! But I knew I needed to check with my neighbors to find out if it belonged to anyone in the neighborhood. I knew the cat would be hungry after a long night in the tree, so I put out a bowl of food and it began eating right away. After it finished eating, I reached down to pet it, the cat was quite friendly and happy for the attention. I looked it over and discovered it was a girl.

Later that day, a friend and I canvased the neighborhood to see if anyone was looking for a young long-haired, orange and white cat. We also posted signs in the neighborhood. I waited a few more days to see if she might go home, but she never left, and no one ever came to claim her.

She appeared healthy but I knew I needed to have her checked out by a veterinarian before letting her into the house and exposing my cat to her. The vet discovered she had a respiratory infection and needed antibiotics, but otherwise she was in good shape. She spent the next week at a friend's house while she recovered.

From the moment she showed up on my front porch, she seemed determined she was home. In spite of all the nasty growls and hisses from my cat, she still seemed to want to come inside and be with us. Much to my surprise and delight, it only took about four days for my cat to relax and begin to accept our new housemate.

She was with me for many wonderful years and helped me through the difficult passing of my other cat, the end of a significant relationship, and two long distance moves, to which she adapted remarkably well. She didn't seem to care where we lived, as long as we were together, she was happy. I still miss her. She'll always be in my heart.

Bringing a stray animal into your home and family

Sometimes a stray animal arrives in your life when you least expect it. Your neighbor brings over a lost dog hoping you'll take it in, your daughter shows up with a cat she found on the way home from school, you discover an abandoned animal on the street or in a parking lot.

Make every attempt to locate the animal's owner; if it has a microchip, finding the owner may be quick and easy, as long as the microchip info is current. If the owner cannot be located, you'll need to decide if the animal will go to a shelter or rescue organization, or if you want to adopt it.

If you consider keeping the animal, think about the need it will fill in your life, and whether you are willing and able to provide everything it needs to be happy and healthy. You also need to consider any current pets and how they may respond to another pet joining the family—especially if your pets have not been exposed to this type of animal.

It is not a good idea to bring a stray or lost animal into your home or expose it to your pets before it's been examined by a veterinarian and tested for disease and parasites. You also don't know how it might respond to your pets.

If you decide to keep the animal, you'll need to write an agreement between you and your new pet. Follow the example agreement which pertains to the type of animal you're taking in.

Writing an agreement between you and a stray pet you've taken in is a positive step you can take toward building a happy, balanced, and healthy relationship. However, the agreement does not guarantee the animal will be a perfect fit for you or your family. Nor does it ensure you or your family will be a perfect fit for the animal.

Here are a few things you need to be aware of and look for once your new pet is living with you

If you already have a pet, pay close attention to how your pet is reacting to and interacting with the new pet. Is your current pet trying to harm the new pet, or is the new pet trying to harm your current pet? You can't expect or force your current pet to accept the new pet, nor can you expect or force the new pet to accept your current pet. Each animal must be willing to accept the other and cohabitate peacefully.

Observe how the new pet interacts with you and family members, and how family members interact with the new pet. Is anyone in the family experiencing allergies to the new pet?

Is the new pet adjusting to you and your family? This is especially important if you have a baby or small children, as not all animals are comfortable with children. It is your responsibility to make sure interaction is safe and positive for the child and the pet.

Is the new pet adjusting to the life you're providing for it? Is it comfortable inside your home and outside, if it spends time outside? Is it eating, sleeping, grooming, and getting into a regular routine? Is it getting enough time for play, exercise, and interaction with you and family members?

Everyone in the family (people and pets) will need time to adjust to the new pet, and your new pet will need time to become comfortable with its new family and life.

Within about four weeks you'll probably have some indication of how things are working between you, family members and your new pet. *It may take up to a year or longer for a pet to become comfortable with you, family members and its environment. Keep this in mind regarding the behaviors, lifestyle, activities or job you would like your pet to learn, accept or tolerate*

About Kelly O'Tillery

Author Kelly O'Tillery has written this guidebook based on her own practical yet groundbreaking technique for an enlightened approach to relating on an emotional and soul level with pets. She combines intuitive and pet communication examples of her work, as she explores the ways she has found are most appreciated by the clients, friends and animals she has connected with in the course of her life. She has lived with pets, enjoyed getting to know a variety of creatures big and small, loved and learned from them and from seeking to create a connection with them.

Kelly introduces an exciting new concept anyone can put into practice in their own relationship with their pet(s), "Using the techniques in this book will help you build an even stronger bond with your pet. You'll gain greater clarity and insight into what you want and expect from your pet, what you're able to provide for your pet and what your pet needs from you."

She continues, "Whether we know it or not, each relationship we have is a reflection of our own spiritual connection with our world. We can all benefit from becoming aware of how important every relationship is, and how significant our role is in them."

website: guidetoahappypet.com
Facebook https://www.facebook.com/guidetoahappypet/
email: guidetoahappypet@gmail.com

Made in the USA
Lexington, KY
02 November 2019